When The World Paused Again:
What a pandemic taught us about living

Various Contributors
Edited by Michelle Gant

Copyright ©2021 Michelle Gant
All rights reserved
ISBN: 9798497942446

This book is dedicated to all the heroes of the pandemic –
the ones we know about, and the ones unsung.

Thank you.

Thank You to: Joanna Playford, Anne Francis, Claire Findlay, Peter Holt, Nicola Pritchard, Charley Purves, Robert Clarke, Stu Haysman, Sauy Li, Vicky Etheridge, DW, Michal Siewniak, Abbie Panks, Helen Hooper, Tom Page, Chris Playford (Dad), Emma O'Shaughnessy, Helen Terry, Donna-Louise Bishop, Ronda Jackson, Stephanie Brighton, Georgina Rouse, Martin Hales, Neil Staveley, Sharon Clifton, Tony Hall, Sarah Dennis, Ange Fox, Serena Grant, Lucy Wigley, Emma Cluett, Hannah Freeman, Lara Laing, Kirsty Jonas, Gill Lawson, Anna Franklin, Alix Young, Alma Sheren, Steph Allen, Jacqueline Fry, Thea Gant (what a star you are sweetheart!), Rosie Walden, Thomas Murray, Clive Bartlett, Janka Robinson, Caroline Fawcett, Sarah Jones, Samantha Slusar, Anna Tydeman, Charlotte Sexton, Jodi Coathup, Johnny Wharton, Claire Smith, Jayne McGurk, Julie Shield, Fiona Buchan, Jo Lake, Stephani Davis, Wendy Gant (Mil), Danielle Warman, Lucy Lawson, Anita Hamer, Liam Weeks, Georgie Holmes, Kate Burrows, Candice Liverpool, Robert Gant, Haze Carver, Gemma Brown, Eddie West-Burnham, Suzanna Wood, Edward Murray, Vicki Haverson, Janet Traynor, Emma Outten, Tom Holt, Eliza Warden, Jamie Backhouse, Donna Stokes, Prabir Mitra, Isabel Varey, Chloe Connor, and Mark Warwick. Thank you so much to you all for sharing your reflections so openly during such a difficult time; your words inspired, uplifted, and motivated me and so many others. Thank you for being amazing.

Thank you to Danielle Warman for designing the brilliant front cover.

Thank you so much to everyone who has shown support for When The World Paused over the last two years, whether reading the blog, buying a book, or helping me to get the word out. From tiny acorns, this magical project has grown. Thank you.

And finally, thank you to my family and friends for all your kindness, your love, and your wise words during the last two years. Above all, thank you to Bobby and Thea for being your wonderful selves and making me grateful every day.

Michelle Gant, November 2021

Introduction

On 23rd March 2020, Prime Minister Boris Johnson announced a 'stay at home' period for at least three weeks in response to the novel coronavirus which was spreading rapidly through the UK and the rest of the world. The announcement followed similar 'lockdowns' across Europe and globally

In fact, the first lockdown lasted rather more than three weeks – it wasn't until June 2020 when the rules were relaxed with non-essential shops able to reopen alongside a phased return to schools. That summer saw further easing. Many of us shared our reflections on this utterly unprecedented time in our first collection of **When The World Paused** reflections. Our book ended with a hope that the pandemic was behind us.

It wasn't.

September 2020 brought sombre warnings of further restrictions as cases began to rise. That autumn saw various measures brought in across the UK including a two-week 'firebreak' lockdown in Wales and a month-long lockdown in England. In addition, tier systems were also introduced allowing for localised restrictions.

Hope came with the roll out of the coronavirus vaccination programme starting in earnest on 8th December 2020. But it was too late to stop the rise of a new variant which brought lockdown and tightened restrictions in January 2021 - restrictions that only began to be eased gradually from spring 2021 onwards.

These are our stories of what happened **When The World Paused Again**, and what we learnt about living in this period of time that we shall never, ever forget.

Tuesday 23rd March 2021, National Day of Reflection: Michelle Gant
Words, once spoken
Whisper in an echo
Scent, once trailed
Time to time will blow
A hand, once placed
Leaves its lasting mark
A face, once seen
Still visible in the dark
A presence, so great
Through memory will endure
A love, so strong
It lasts forever more.

Monday 29th March 2021: Michelle Gant
And they thought it was all over.

Exactly one year ago today, I started a journal to capture the reflections of people when the world paused. Lockdown had just begun in the UK as the novel coronavirus wound its devastating way across the world. I was, like so many others, frightened, uncertain, anxious, and trying to find sense and meaning in the most incredulous period I had ever known.

Writing, I thought, would help. Not only would it allow me to capture the reflections of this moment – which felt imbued with future historical significance – it would also enable me to process my thoughts and feelings in words. It turned out this wouldn't be a secret diary though as 75 other amazing people joined me in sharing their innermost musings.

That journal closed in June 2020 and I turned it into a book to raise funds for NHS charities. It felt like a neat ending; I like things to be ordered. I like too to be able to find the good in any situation, and it certainly felt like through the journal, and subsequent book, that had been achieved.

But it turned out that it wasn't 'the end', and as the Chief Medical Officer had said, it was merely the end of the first phase.

There was more to come.

It was September 2020 when the alarm started to buzz. Cases rising. *Cases? People.* Mutterings of second waves. I am, by nature, a woman who drinks from a half-filled glass (of wine, often) and so I tried not to be too concerned. *Things will work out,* I told myself. *It will be all right. We'll be back together by Christmas.*

But then things got worse and in November 2020 we had our second lockdown. Albeit with the schools still open – thank goodness our children didn't have to give up their newly found classroom freedom. When we came out of it, my part of the world was in 'tier two' which meant restrictions were a little looser than in other parts of the country. It was ok. I could still see my loved ones. Even if it wasn't close up.

And then something magical happened.

Question: What is Margaret Keenan famous for?

This was a query I posed in our virtual Christmas Day quiz. And the answer is quite magnificently – she is the very first person in the UK to receive the coronavirus vaccination. On Tuesday 8th December 2020, I cried as I watched the images of this 90-year-old lady receive a shot in the arm, a significant victory in the battle against the virus. *It was actually happening. Thank you scientists. Thank you NHS.*

But what's the saying? The night is always darkest just before the dawn. Because then things got bad. Really bad.

A new variant, easier to catch. Spreading with speed across the country, particularly in the East of England. *That's my area. Gulp.* Tightened restrictions, and then on 4th January 2021, another lockdown was announced.

Oh my.

We've been here before. It's ok. We've got this.

We have.

Only, this time, it's winter. The days are dark and cold. The news is scary, the numbers of people affected higher. The novelty of lockdown activities of baking, and crafts, of appreciating the time to do and try new things has long since worn off.

This lockdown felt like wading through thick, murky fog.

It was the *fear*. As acutely demonstrated by a covid test for my poorly and distressed daughter Thea at the start of the year, and the suggestion from medical staff that she had caught the dreaded virus. "But we haven't been anywhere," I bemoaned, plaintively. The kindly lady on the phone just murmured in agreement: it didn't matter, this strain could reach you however careful you were. Thank goodness, she was negative (and eating ice-cream again within hours).

It was the *sadness. Those losses*. As I type, over 126,000 people in this country have died with Covid-19. The pain of those left behind is unfathomable. May they find comfort.

It was the *missing*. This past week we marked one year since the first lockdown with a national day of reflection. I realised it's well over a year since I've hugged my parents or my sisters or my friends.

It was the *weariness*. It's just so exhausting, trying to keep hopeful and positive when waves of bad news and negativity keep washing up onto your shore. I hit a low point around February half term when I just felt so tired and defeated with trying to offer Thea anything but my dodgy arts and crafts by way of entertainment. Which brings me onto......

It was the *guilt*. The constant nagging feeling that I wasn't doing enough, worrying about the impact of all of this on poor little Thea. When she said to me: "I don't like the video calls. I just want to 'huggle' people," I felt so proud of her eloquent self-awareness, and terrible that her little arms ached so for those she loves.

But.

Whilst there has been so much awfulness in the last year, there has been so much good stuff too. And a pandemic has taught me so many things about living.

Firstly, life is happening. Right now. And even when it's not shaped the way you'd hope, it's there for the living. Grab on to it, and carpe the diem out of it. That was why for my birthday earlier this month I had an amazing virtual party – I found myself saying "next year, I'll have a party." "Next year," doesn't exist. But now, right here, does. So, squeeze every drop of pleasure out of it that you possibly can.

And life isn't certain. In any way shape or form. So just go with it. Accept it as it is in all its mixed up, confused glory and who knows what nuggets of gold you might find down amongst the dirt.

Fears are there to be overcome. Over the last year, the most frightening one I've known, I've come to realise that what scares us should never defeat us. I'm not fearless, I still have things that frighten me, but I know that I can deal with *anything*. It's why this year I've started trying to do one thing out of my comfort zone every day.

You don't need to sit beside people to feel close to them. The two-metre rule has not prevented me from feeling connected to more people than ever before: we're all in this thing together. There has been so much virtual looking out for each other that has brought us closer.

That we are capable of so much more than we can ever conceive. Like my husband Bobby, who has been an absolute home-schooling hero, devoting himself every lockdown weekday to our daughter's education with tender attention and care.

And the things that I always thought mattered, the material stuff, bears little value to that which is really important in my world.

Today marks a further easing of the restrictions. Six people can now meet up outside together. And hopefully this is another step on the road towards a resumption – of a fashion – of our former lives.

So, one more time, we're going to capture what happened when the world paused, and look ahead as we share our thoughts on what a pandemic taught us about living…..

Tuesday 30th March 2021: Joanna Playford

On the evening of 23rd of March 2020, Prime Minister Boris Johnson announced a national lockdown due to the outbreak of Covid-19. A year on and we are now in a third lockdown and I am still working from home in my job as a travel agent; I initially thought home working would be just for a few weeks. I have adjusted to working from home having found it difficult and stressful to begin with: I no longer dread the day ahead. With a road map out of lockdown in sight and shops reopening, I will return to the office in the next couple of weeks although it will not be the quite the same with social distancing needing to be adhered too. I am not sure when the fab four (this is what I call our team) will be reunited at our shop but I hope that it is not too long; my colleagues will be pleased to know that I now know how to make tea.

After a year of little or no travel, future travel is now looking more positive with the roll out of the vaccines. The travel industry still faces a challenging few months ahead, and we wait to hear when we can travel safely again. I long for the day when I see planes in the sky and the obligatory beach selfies on Instagram. After a year of re-bookings and cancellations, it seems we have weathered the storm, and are now seeing new bookings both in the UK and overseas.

In 2020 I turned 40. It was not the big birthday that I had planned. There was no party and no big celebration. It was a quiet affair with just my partner and me. A very special holiday was cancelled. I saw on TV yesterday that if you turned a milestone in 2020 then it doesn't count. If that is the case, I am still 39 and will be celebrating my birthday this year in the Maldives (hopefully).

Being at home for most of the year has meant I have put the dreaded Covid stone in weight on. Having had my head in the fridge for most of the year and a bottle of wine never very far from my grasp, I am now actively exercising; I've even downloaded an app onto my phone.

Things that I have learnt about myself....
- I still can't cook;
- I am addicted to online shopping (Zara and Asos sales must have soared with my orders);
- I have really bad hair and I'm in desperate need of a haircut/colour;
- I binge on reality TV (Married at First Sight Australia has got me through the long evenings);
- I miss my family and can't wait to hug and kiss my niece and nephew.

In what has been a really difficult year, I do believe there is light at the end of the tunnel. And yesterday was a good day - I received my first vaccine.

Wednesday 31ˢᵗ March 2021: Anne Francis

Who would have thought that the world could change so much in so short a time? As I write this, we are just emerging from the third lockdown, the sun is shining, and I'm overwhelmed with gratitude for the many silver linings that the last year has brought with it.

A year ago, my dad had just been diagnosed with Alzheimer's disease and I was taking him for daily walks. Now he walks slowly and painfully with a frame and the long, cold, dark, tough winter put paid to any outdoor activity. Family have rallied round, one of the silver linings is that we are closer, more understanding and kinder to each other. I see this shift reflected in wider society too. The boxes of random free stuff left outside people's houses, the volunteer networks, the sharing skills online, the checking in with each other and sending love/food/books when someone is struggling.

Learning to ask for help when I've struggled has been a personal shift that I'm now quite proud of.

This year I've also learned to make gnocchi, cut my own hair, grow sweetcorn and cucumbers, start a new business and have even sorted my toolbox. I've read a lot of books, discovered Feldenkrais, 'Zoom meeting-ed' a bit and entered the best bubble ever.

Decades of self-employment have made me pretty resilient and able to weather the uncertainties of life. The last year tested me to the limit and I think I'm emerging generally a little more appreciative, accepting, mindful, and discerning.

Today has been an example of a day that perhaps I would have taken for granted before covid. Breakfast under a tree in the cemetery with a dear friend, off to my bubble to look after one year old Milo for the afternoon, more walking in the woods, buying vegetable seeds from a local garden centre, picking up four-year-old Dexter from nursery, sharing a meal then putting him to bed. Arriving home to write this, a box of wonderful organic veg waiting for me. Simple pleasures which for the first three months of lockdown were not all possible. The worst of times was that first lockdown and not being able to hug loved ones. It was the best of feelings to belong to a bubble.

The three lockdowns have all had their own qualities, for me, the last one going through the winter was the hardest but even in the darkest hours I managed to find comfort in the connections with family, friends, and nature.

Looking after my parents has been a privilege and I've had more time for them as my bed and breakfast closed in March 2020. The piecemeal work I've been doing since then pays the bills and leaves me flexible with time. As my parents enter the winter of their lives, I am able to draw strength from the experiences of last year and know that we kept them safe, and we did our best.

So, my pace of life has slowed somewhat and I'm happy to be a homebody. I now know every bird that lives and visits my garden and every cat! I only go into the city centre to pick up books from my favourite book shop the Book Hive and I'm making do and mending a lot more than I used to.

Thank goodness for internet shopping and I'm gently getting myself ready to step back into the world again. Back to work, back to non-essential shopping, back to cafes and restaurants, back to sharing food round a table with friends (but not yet!) and back to travelling.

Thursday 1st April 2021: Claire Findlay

April Fool's Day is with us again. There is a little more room for laughter this year and the hope that there is much more to be had as we move forward in this new world.

What a year it has been since I wrote my reflections for 'When the World Paused' in 2020. It was a shock a year ago that we had succumbed to a lockdown but here we are again in lockdown three. Little did we know back then that this pandemic was going to be with us for this long but hopefully we are getting through it and at least the lifting of some restrictions on our route map out of lockdown are giving us hope that we are heading towards some kind of 'normality', whatever that may look like in our new world. The vaccination programme in the UK is proving to be successful so far. I am still waiting for mine as I type but I'm hoping I'm not too far down the list now.

It has certainly been a year for reflection and adapting to a new way of living. For me there has been so much new learning and new opportunities that may not have occurred if it hadn't been for the lockdowns and restrictions. For this, I am grateful.

There has been a new sense of respect for our NHS, emergency services and education staff that may have been absent before. People have given more, whether it is time or physical things, without expecting anything in return.

Last year I reflected on my different roles as a person in this world so I thought I would update this.

As a mum, I am so proud of my daughter, Esmé. She had a bad start to 2020 and missed a lot of school and was faced with uncertainty of what her future may hold. She moved schools in September 2020 for her last academic school year (Year 11). I wasn't convinced that this move would be good but she has proved to us all that this was the best decision. She has found new friends and a new love for learning. Despite not knowing whether she would be sitting exams and having a disrupted year of education she has shown resilience and got stuck into her learning and made massive improvements. She seems to be in a much happier place and has high hopes for her future and is looking forward with enthusiasm and that is all we can ask.

As a wife, again nothing much has changed. I am used to the other half working at home now. It can be annoying not having the house to myself as I have had before when I'm on school breaks but on a positive note it makes me go outside more.

As a daughter I have had mixed emotions. My mum and dad continued to have a rough time with their health. They were forced into staying at home throughout this pandemic and worst of all not seeing us, their family, or friends as much as they should. The one positive thing that has happened for them this year was that they finally got Wi-Fi. This was a blessing as we could finally video call and see each other. It was particularly nice when Esmé put on a mini concert for my birthday this year and we could share it with them too. This will be a happy memory I will treasure forever.

My job as a teacher has completely changed and this has continued to be the biggest challenge for me. We have had no heads up and have been acting upon regular government information and advice given to us at the same time as the rest of the UK population. We started the new school year with some restrictions in place. Lockdown two didn't really change too much for us as school continued as 'normal'. Then came January 2021, back in lockdown and remote learning was in place once more. This time around we felt a bit more prepared. We still had families questioning the key worker places and we had an increase in the number of children attending school than in the first lockdown so all staff were needed in school, no rotas for us this time. Connecting with our children and families remained crucial. This time around we started using

Zoom meetings with our classes. These turned out to be good fun, bringing the children learning in school and at home together, learning through games was key. We also provided a lot more recorded lessons and activities for the children to access as well as home learning packs.

Our job was considerably harder as we were having to split our teaching time between those in school and those at home as well as planning and completing welfare checks with all our families and all the other unseen jobs a teacher does. The first couple of weeks were great but as time went on we could sense the frustration from families who were trying to juggle home schooling, their own work, and general things that we all just need to do in life. Home wasn't home for some anymore - it had become a school and a workplace with no escape. The winter months didn't help the mood either as people felt trapped inside unlike in the first lockdown where we at least had the warmer weather that helped lift spirits and when we could get outside. I am so grateful for the team of lovely people I work with, we really do support each other through the toughest of times and lift each other's spirits when needed.

The five ways to wellbeing have been a huge help to me over the last year.

Connecting
This one has been essential in the last year when meeting people in person has been restricted. Even though we couldn't see many people in person video calling has become a necessity. What was great in the latter part of last year we finally managed to get my mum and dad set up with tablets so we could see them as well as talk over the phone. When restrictions allowed us, we went to see Mum and Dad on Christmas Day and Esmé observed she was the only teenager in the room but the only one NOT on technology! This made us all chuckle with a little bit of guilt at the times we had told her to get off her tech!

It has been a time for being more honest and thoughtful with our words. There have been more 'Love Yous' shared as a result and things said that may not have been said if we carried on with our busy lives. We now know, more than ever the true value of the spoken and typed word and how much it means to us all as individuals.

Esmé and I make sure we spend time together each day. This can be watching TV, eating dinner, sharing Tik Toks or YouTube videos. One memorable time we spent together was watching a fantastic series called 'The Good Doctor'. We made time in the evenings to watch this together and this soon became our new time together. This programme made us laugh and cry together but it was quality time.

We have had plenty of Zoom quizzes to attend which have been great fun too. Connecting with people on a quiz night from London, Canada and Tennessee, USA and Cleethorpes, UK, has made Saturday night entertainment have a new meaning.

Connecting with others by contributing to this journal last year and this year, the subsequent published book to raise money for the NHS, and then recording my reflections and sharing for the local radio station has been amazing. Thank you, Michelle, for making this all possible. I've learnt that it is good to write down my thoughts.

Give
I love to help others so being able to volunteer and support others helped me enormously. I volunteered early on in the first lockdown doing welfare checks on others in need and delivering prescriptions and shopping to those shielding and staying at home.

Supporting friends and family is also important to me and by just giving up some of my time to be that listening ear when someone has needed it gives me some self-satisfaction.

There has been an abundance of people 'giving' whether it be their time, donations of food, support, and love. People have put out boxes of unwanted items like puzzles, books, and toys for others to reuse.

Supporting local business has become more important to me so where I can I look to shop locally rather than online.

Having a purpose in this world is important to me and if I can help somebody else just that little bit to make their life a little bit easier I find rewarding.

Take Notice
I love that people have got to know their local community more and have taken time to speak to and check in with their neighbours. We are certainly very lucky with our little bunch of 'Hazel Grovies'!

This last year has allowed me to reflect and spend time on me without feeling that guilt. Although I haven't got much fitter I have definitely walked more steps than usual and taken time to do the things that I enjoy doing most.

I have enjoyed taking the time noticing the seasonal changes more and much of this has been done through my love of walking. I even had some very early starts so that I could appreciate the sun rising out of the sea on our beautiful Norfolk coastline.

I have taken more time to learn about the collection of essential oils I have and their benefits and these have certainly played a part in my positive wellbeing.

Keep Learning
I love learning new things especially if it is going to be useful to

my everyday life. It has definitely been a year of new learning for me. The use of technology must be the biggest. Recording lessons and stories for the children in my class learning at home, creating online quizzes for family and friends. Teaching my mum and dad how to use their tablets. All of these things have required 'thinking out of the box' skills which I love to challenge myself with. If you could see the creative ways we balanced the iPads to record different teaching activities, just to get the right angle I'm sure you would be quite amused.

Opportunities to do some online learning to support my job have definitely been a positive way forward. I have invested a lot of my time focusing on my knowledge about mental health this year. Learning at your own pace in the comfort of your own home is definitely a bonus. The mute and stop video have had their uses too.

I have even learnt a few little life hacks from Tik Tok! It is amazing what you can learn if you look for the opportunities. Experimenting with cooking has always been something I like but having more time to spend on it has brought me new satisfaction.

I have decided to start a new business promoting natural beauty products that I use and love. This is something I would never have considered doing but a very good friend gave me a nudge in the right direction so that will bring lots of new learning and opportunities my way.

The most important thing is learning about 'me' and having the time for self-care without feeling the guilt.

Be Active
Being outside is something I love the most. I love watching the seasonal changes and observing what each one brings. We have discovered many new walks from our doorstep and some a short drive away that we had never done before. I love taking a

new path and exploring what new adventures it can offer. Our dog Betsy loves exploring new places too. Having her in our lives has ensured we get out walking more. She has been a huge asset to our family and in particular to our mental health and wellbeing. She is my BFF (Best Furry Friend).

This time last year I was busy planting some vegetables. It was rewarding harvesting the few things I planted and using the produce for meals. Again, this year I find myself repeating that task, adapting to what did and didn't work last year.

I find that all these five ways interlink as part of my everyday life and have become a way of being that is essential for my mental health and wellbeing.

Today I was able to do a little bit of all five of these steps. I went for a lovely walk with a dear friend. She took me on a new walk, away from the hustle and bustle and around the quiet countryside which we both love and appreciate so much. We observed the beautiful primroses that appeared to be blossoming at their best this year and the little purple violets pushing their way through. I saw my first lamb of the year and some baby squirrels scurrying around. The birds were full of song and were busy building their nests ready for their young. Spring is one of my favourite seasons. I love that it represents new beginnings and the start of new life.

I sadly lost my dad last week, after a long battle of illness. Even though expected it happened far quicker than we thought. I was able to reflect on his life journey with the trust that there was a listening ear and somebody who understood my loss. My friend had known my dad too but through different eyes but she described him as 'Twinkly'. This made me smile as I knew exactly what she meant. He was always wanting to help others and make others smile, nothing was too much trouble and he loved nothing more than to make others around him happy.

My friend was one of many recipients of these characteristics from my dad. We have received many messages from the people that knew my dad that have confirmed what we knew and that has been of huge comfort to us during this sad time. I like to think that I am my dad and share those wonderful human qualities, he taught me well. I feel privileged that I was able to give something back to him and care for him along with my sister in the last 24 hours of his life and that he could pass peacefully at home where he wanted to be surrounded by his family who loved him.

This pandemic hasn't gone on without its challenges and frustrations but together we have found a new a way of living and being. I am aware that people will have processed this new world differently, some people will have had moments where they were falling apart, some have had their hearts broken through the loss of a loved one, some will have found the strength and held it together and some will not know how this has affected them for some time to come but that this is all ok as we are all different and doing the best we can in our own way for now. I know I have personally been on an emotional rollercoaster. It is important that we continue to check in with each other regardless.

I continue to tell myself that all of this is all happening for a reason. We could focus on what we may have missed out on, but I believe it has given us the time to reflect on what we do have and to show more gratitude for the little things and adapt where necessary. I like to think that this is not a new way of living for me but just confirmed what I already believed. I hope that many will find positivity and gratitude from this last year despite the challenges it has given us all.

Stay safe everyone and continue to follow the guidance and hopefully we can continue to move along this route map with hope. Life might not be the same as it was, but we can all find some happiness in what it will be, if we all look hard enough.

Friday 2nd April 2021: Peter Holt

I wrote a year ago, at that time ten days into lockdown, that I was hunkering down for the long-haul. I am pretty sure that what I meant at the time was maybe until the early autumn, and certainly not for over a year - so I'd count that one in the naive optimism column.

I got my first jab in February 2021 in the end, and at the time, that felt like a very early privilege.

A year ago, I wrote that I hoped to move back to Newcastle one day. Well, I managed that last summer - I thought that if I'm going to be 'shielding', and working remotely, I might as well do it 200 miles from the office in my own home, instead of 100 yards away in a rented home.

So here we are - and according to official Government advice, I was able to stop shielding from yesterday, and see a handful of people outside. Seeing as I live on the 11th floor, there's not a whole lot of garden-gathering going on in my life - but still, at least I can play tennis again, which is an absolute godsend.

One big difference that the pandemic has made to me is that I stayed in my job maybe a lot longer than I would have done otherwise. The odd opportunity did come up, but in general I figured that lockdown wasn't a great time to try changing jobs. At least I still had a steady income, and a job that I was well geared up to do remotely - after all, our office was closed, so there wasn't much of an expectation that I'd be physically present.

My job was a fixed term contract though, and after three years that came to an end two days ago, so I have entered the remote job-hunting market after all.

My experience so far: it hasn't made much of a difference, to me at least. Obviously, the process was different - I went through one long and elaborate multi-stage recruitment process that culminated the week before last. Lots of remote interviews, stakeholder sessions, and psychometric tests. I didn't get that job in the end - they slept on it between me and the other candidate and went with them the next morning.

Close but no banana. Onwards and upwards.

I figure that maybe I lost the edge just a little in that if I'd been in the room, I'd have been able to make a bit more of a positive impression through lots of direct eye contact, reading the room, conveying my energy and so on - but pretty marginal to be honest. I have though never been less nervous for a big interview than I was online.

Another thing I wrote a year ago that definitely deserves its place in the naive optimism column: that I was determined to come out of lockdown as #fitpetenotfatpete. Well - my weight has been pretty stable, but I can't pretend I'm any fitter.

I improvised a home workout station, in the absence of the gym - but it's not been the four times a week habit I'd hoped for. And jogging stopped in the autumn to be honest - once I gave in and admitted that it was a joyless trudge for me. Tennis is my great hope at aerobic resurrection though.

From my 11th floor vantage point, and in my strolls through the city centre and down the Tyne, I've got a much clearer idea of how the world has shut down. All those city centre shops and restaurants not just closed but stripped out.

Kudos to my local council though - pedestrianisation and animation plans so that the city centre can grow back differently as a destination, not just crossing its fingers and hoping that units will magically find new tenants. God knows what is going to happen to the big Top Shop store though, and the even bigger empty Debenhams.

I can't say that my mental health has always been peachy through a year of lockdown. Living alone has its merits, and I thank God that I'm not home schooling anyone, but a reliance on Zoom for personal interaction has been somewhat less than ideal. I figure though that us natural introverts are perhaps better suited to social distancing.

Grumpy that I'm not skiing at the moment, as that is my usual Easter pastime, but I'm not so detached from reality as to realise that this definitely counts as yet another #firstworldproblem.

Oh, and yes, I now bake my own bread. Clichéd, but glorious!

Saturday 3rd April 2021: Nicola Pritchard
We've clapped, we've cheered, we've donated, and we've cried!!!

And here we are a year on, slowly easing out of our third lockdown.

And here I am counting down the days till I can go back to work as a hairdresser, back to some form of normality.

Although some days have seemed long and not so bright, this past year a lot has changed - believe it or not in a positive way. Since the first lockdown back in March 2020, I have taken up yoga and running; not only has this been good for me physically but also good for my mental health, and I will carry on doing this. My husband Simon was still able to work (which I am very grateful for, and all that he has done for us). So, my days have been spent with our 4-year-old son Harley - being his mummy, his cleaner, and best of all, his play mate. The current thing he loves doing is looking for worms in our garden for his wormery which my dad brought for him for Christmas (a book or toy would have been just fine). We are very fortunate to have some beautiful walks and woodlands where we live so we have spent a lot of time exploring, going on bike rides. We've definitely made a lot of lovely memories - just shows you the best things in life are free.

At the end of last year I celebrated my 40th and Harley celebrated turning four. Who says you can't party hard even if it is just the three of us, Harley had the best birthday and I have to say he is a better dancer than me. We would have loved to have had all our friends and family to celebrate with us but hopefully next birthday will be different.

There was a downside to last year - our honeymoon was cancelled which I was disappointed about, something I had been looking forward to for nearly a year. But we have booked a family holiday in this country later this year. I also missed my family, friends, and work; being a hairdresser your clients become your friends too. Most of all I have felt sorry for Harley. I was worried that as he hadn't been able to interact with other children, he would be nervous about going back to nursery after such a long time away. How wrong was I! I am so proud of him, he has been such a good boy and has settled back into nursery as if he hasn't been away. He doesn't understand Covid but he understands that people are poorly. And now most days he asks: "Are people better yet?" and "Can we go to the dinosaur park yet?"

Tonight, I raise my glass to all the people who have sadly passed away, and to all my family and friends. And I'm grateful for all we have. Stay positive, be kind…and as a wise man once said: "Tomorrow will be a better day".

Sunday 4th April 2021: Charley Purves

Happy Easter! A day that Christians across the world rejoice and celebrate the risen Christ. My faith has often waivered, and I've never felt a particularly strong pull to the church. But I was brought up Roman Catholic and over the years I have grown to appreciate the community that surrounds our parish – where people know me and my family, that are always looking out for us.

Pre-Covid we would attend mass most Sundays and parish events, as well as the Community Kitchen on a Tuesday lunchtime when I was on maternity leave. My boys were a hit with both the volunteers and the attendees alike – John was often passed round for cuddles and William would play with whoever gave him a smile! I feel so much gratitude for having been able to experience this and feel so much for those that relied on going for support and a hot meal they may not have otherwise had. How are they coping now? I really hope they are well.

But now I do feel much closer to God and feel a great deal of contentment having been to church. I will also more readily pray now, feeling that connection.

This past year has turned everyone's lives upside down. My mental health has always been somewhat fragile and there have been times over these last few months that I have really struggled. The coronacoaster has been real!

I remember what can only be described as an adrenaline rush as we were launched into this unreal world, suddenly working from home and having to ensure that our team had all the equipment they needed to continue their work, particularly those who were suddenly taking calls from distressed business owners. I can only imagine how traumatic that was. My husband was furloughed which meant he could look after the boys while I tried to work as best I could from our bedroom.

I was playing Harry Potter at this point – making no noise and pretending I wasn't there! Because if they heard me, they would want to come in and play.

But along with that adrenaline, was also fear and anxiety and I dip in and out of moments of pure depression. Right now, I am feeling ok. I can't imagine life without social restrictions, and I can't get my brain into gear for making plans. My brain works in overdrive and I overthink everything. I also keep losing my words – which makes writing this a real challenge. But on the whole I feel ok. The sun has been shining this week and we are able to get out and do things again – some positivity.

We formed a support bubble with my mum as soon as we were able to. With her being on her own and us only being five minutes down the road, as opposed to my sister an hour away, this made sense. She really is my rock and I don't know how I would cope without her. We've been able to keep some sense of normality in this respect, so much so, we slept over at hers last night and after mass this morning, spent the day playing in the garden and enjoyed a roast beef dinner this afternoon.

We also met my sister and her family yesterday for a walk and picnic – the first time the five cousins (my two boys and her three girls!) have been together in many months. It was so wonderful to see them playing together and of course they have all grown so much. John is now interacting with them a lot more and it was lovely to see him running around and playing so freely with them. He is so fiercely independent but can also be quite shy and clingy.

William started school last September and he has absolutely flourished. We were lucky that he wasn't at school during that first lockdown, but it has meant we've had to get used to schooling during a pandemic – something he won't know any different – but we have not been able to go into his classroom or see his first nativity. He has made such lovely friendships and has really done well with learning to read, write and count. He is an absolute sponge! His confidence has grown so much too, taking part in things I didn't think he would be interested in. He's desperate to get back to gymnastics and swimming so let's hope we can manage it soon.

I feel strangely jealous of those who have found new hobbies or done great things during this pandemic. I have put on a number of lockdown pounds and was drinking too much. But I've made a conscious effort since the start of the year to curb this and move more. I started yoga again, but I'm still trying to get into a groove with any other activity. My husband, Doug, on the other hand has started cycling again and is cycling to work on a regular basis.

Of the things that have changed for us, I really hope that our green credentials will continue to improve. We're not relying on our cars quite so much and enjoying staying close to home and using local shops. We need to get our garden and vegetable patch sorted so we can also enjoy our home-grown food. We've also started reducing our plastic waste too, and recycling items we can't put in normal recycling.

I hope everyone can take something positive out of this time and have something they can focus on going forward – into a brighter and better time.

Monday 5th April 2021: Robert Clarke
Part 1

I first began writing this piece whilst sitting in the dining room with the sun streaming through the windows and the daffodils and other spring flowers looking fantastic in the garden. I am really now beginning to feel optimistic about the rest of the year.

Sadly, sometimes our optimism gets kicked back – with the news that we are to expect wintry weather imminently! A minor blip in the context of the last year, I hope. Let's see what happens?

Over the last year I think we have become accustomed to taking several steps forward and then having to then step back for a while - but that's how life is at the moment. We have all had to adapt and change our lifestyles in some ways.

On my last note of sadness, I am having to let go of my faithful walking boots. We have been together for a while now but the last year of constant walking during the various lockdowns has meant that last week, I had to purchase a new replacement pair. Today, will probably be one of our last trips out – we have covered many countless miles walking the streets, beaches, and woodlands.

I wonder how many of us will continue with the regular walking experiences over the next 12 months or so? Personally, the pleasure I have had experiencing the outdoors throughout all the seasons has helped to keep me grounded.

I feel I have been very lucky to have still been able to go socially distanced fishing for most of the pandemic. Meeting up with friends most weeks to share thoughts and stories has helped give me a focus. I have found it very therapeutic. We say we are not competitive but I know different! You cannot beat healthy competition.

Last week we were able to spend a few hours with the two grandchildren. Fortunately, they have been able to continue with schooling as their mum is a frontline worker. They appear just to be getting on with life as they know it and although we have not seen them for a while we soon settled back to where we were.

Part 2
Just back from my last trip out with my faithful boots. What sprung to mind while I was visiting Holkham Hall was the subject of trust. It was our first trip out where we have experienced having a lot of people around us. I felt we could trust the people that were in the grounds as their behaviour was spot on. Everyone was abiding by the rules and enjoying themselves as couples or larger family groups. It does not take a lot to consider others while out and about. It makes you wonder why some of the human behaviour we have witnessed over the periods of the pandemic has been so selfish – *it isn't difficult to be nice and consider others.*

To continue with the theme of trust, my wife, Davina offered to cut my hair this afternoon (it must have been looking bad). She had purchased some special new scissors and as I was in a trusting mood, we went for it and to be fair the result is very passable. There was not a drop of blood to be seen.

I am now retiring my old trusty walking boots and tomorrow I will be stepping out and forward with the new pair – best foot forward and all that stuff.

I am optimistic that this time next year I will not be replacing my boots again!!

Tuesday 6th April 2021: Stu Haysman

It's the first day back to work after the Easter break. The chocolate egg supply is dwindling fast, snow is lying on the ground and the back-to-back Carry On marathons are at an end (ooohhh Matron - whilst they are massively politically incorrect by modern standards, they are a snapshot in time of British culture and I love them for that). I've spent this morning on a construction site, reviewing safety arrangements for a client, dodging the snow showers, and holding my closing meeting with them before coming home to switch gears and write my reflections.

I thought it was appropriate to start preparing these reflections by reading back over what I wrote a year ago. Doing this was surprisingly triggering actually - words can contain real power can't they? Back then, I compared anxiety to a persistent little terrier, ever-present and always snapping at your heels whenever you let your guard down. He was barking loudly indeed this time last year.

Taking my Anxiety Terrier out again for a little walk quickly brought back how I felt at the start of the pandemic in 2020. It focused me back on the fear I felt then of what might be to come over the next twelve months - medically, emotionally, and financially. But despite that dark feeling, a year has passed, I'm still here, still pushing forwards and surprisingly (for me at least) feeling very optimistic about the future. As it happens, no real long lasting medical or financial damage was done to me or my nearest and dearest and all of the whirling anxieties were mostly smoke and mirrors. I realise how lucky I am.

There have been continuing worries for sure - how to keep my work flowing, how to retain clients, how to earn money, how to look after my friends and family if they get sick, how to cope if the UK toilet roll supply runs out… But anxiety is there to warn us about what *might* happen in the future, not what *is* happening now or *will* definitely happen. My anxiety terrier gets things wrong. It gets things wrong a lot actually. I don't hold that against him - he's trying to protect me after all - but I do know that I shouldn't take what he says as gospel. Not every bark signifies a cobra in the long grass. Rather than taking the barking at face value, it's proved better to engage with the anxious feelings, trying to figure out where they are coming from and whether they are actually logical and likely to come true or not (spoiler - they are probably not either of these things...).

That's all lovely of course, but when engaging with the terrier becomes too much (and it does frequently), a healthy distraction and change of pace is in order.

One of the biggest therapies for me has been indulging in creativity. Those that know me will know that I'm a total hobby hummingbird, flitting from one hobby flower to another, rarely stopping for long. Friends have standing jokes about it, it really is that bad! Maybe I have the pandemic to thank, but taking more time out to sit and think has crystallised my love of pottery and photography. I've been doing lots of both - doing them, reading about them, thinking about them, and even musing on ways I might be able to do them for a living one day instead of the 'day job'.

I'm no Rankin or Grayson Perry of course, but for me, making things puts me into a wonderful flow state and sends the terrier to sleep very quickly indeed (look up Mihaly Csikszentmihalyi to find out about flow). It provides me with a great space to disconnect from day-to-day life for a while and has a surprisingly long-lasting effect.

When you're in it, right up to your neck in it, it can be hard to see positive outcomes sometimes, because we're not clairvoyants are we (unless you are of course, but then you knew I was going to say that...). The pandemic has reminded me that it's totally possible to *believe* things will work out ok, even if you have absolutely no clue how or when it will all come good. The best thing to do when wading through the swamp is to keep wading, even if the leeches, mosquitos, and sulphurous mud are sucking your positivity away! What else are you going to do for goodness sake - stay neck-deep and wait it out?

Wednesday 7th April 2021: Sauy Li

What a bizarre year! What was so new and unprecedented a year ago has become so familiar that it almost seems weirdly normal – this new world of masks, social distancing, working from home, furlough, bubbles, home schooling, Zoom and so much else.

Like the end of most of my days I am at home with the radio for company. My days have become very simple and I have settled into a loose routine after four months in lockdown. It is unbelievable this time has passed, sometimes at a snail's pace and at other times leaving me in a daze as to where the time has gone and what I have done with it.

And what have I done with this past year? Has it really been a full year since I wrote last year's reflections on life in lockdown? Are we really in lockdown v3? It is so difficult to get my head round this year that I don't even know where to begin.

This time last year I was a freelance chef fearing the unknown and worrying about the future of hospitality. The industry is still very uncertain and there are worrying times ahead but I was fortunate to find work and security by taking a permanent position back in August. Thankfully, I have been furloughed throughout this period which has been a real relief. Even though some restrictions will ease next week I will still have to while away my time for another month. The restaurant where I work has decided not to re-open til May. It makes sense as April is known for showers and considering some parts of the UK saw snow only a few days ago the weather is as uncertain as this pandemic. I think I said in my last reflections that I believe we are social beings and I still very much believe that. After being house bound for all these months I think people will want to connect with family and friends and what better way to do this than eating and drinking? I imagine, like me, most people will welcome being cooked for and not having to clear up! It may be different than pre-Covid times and social distancing may still have to be adhered to for a bit longer but it will be great to celebrate again. Together.

For me, this third lockdown has been the toughest and the longest. The first few months were extremely difficult till I realised what I needed was a routine since I was no longer working. It didn't need to be particularly productive or ordered but I did need to get out of hibernation mode. I had lost any inclination for DIY or building flat pack furniture which saw me through much of the second lockdown. To break lockdown fatigue I was able to return to Suffolk at the beginning of February in a bubble and stay with family. It was strange to be giving Christmas presents months afterwards but it was also wonderful to be able to do this. Joining a bubble was a much-needed break from being in my own head space. I was glad I had this time doing everyday things that I had clearly missed like having conversations over a morning coffee, watching TV, enjoying a beer, and sitting round a dinner table in the company of others.

Technology has been a great way to stay connected once I returned to London and being on my own. As well as virtual coffees and cocktail evenings I have randomly enjoyed a McDonald's with my niece on New Year's Day (timing on us getting back from the drive-through was essential!) and going to a virtual gig with a friend on a Saturday was a great night in. As well as practising qigong on a regular basis, I have now added Joe Wicks to my You Tube viewings. Like so many thousands I have started to exercise regularly using his home routines making time pass that much quicker. I guess I have never walked so much as I have this past year whether on my own or with a friend. I now look forward to takeaway Fridays after a long walk, catching up with a friend in Richmond Park, laughing at how we got lost that first time. This has all been good for my mental and physical wellbeing. I have enjoyed being outside even in the winter months as I have watched many beautiful sunsets and warmed my hands on numerous takeaway coffees. Reading and listening to music has really got me through long days and receiving unexpected gifts in the post has often put a smile on my face. I am much happier that the days are now lighter and longer and hopefully warmer and sunnier.

It is these simple pleasures that I hope I will remember and continue to treasure and hopefully practice even when the bustle of life resumes in the coming weeks and months. It seems there is definitely light at the end of the tunnel and there is so much to be grateful for.

Thursday 8th April 2021: Vicky Etheridge

Wow! A whole year since I wrote my first reflections on life in the time of covid, it feels both like six months and six years ago! I wasn't quite sure where to start with this one, I expected something revelatory and 'big' to come to mind and then I realised one of the most important things that I've learnt is…..

It's the little things that matter the most - appreciating the little things was one of my top five tips for surviving lockdown a year ago. I now realise that it is the little things that bring me greatest happiness every day: the weather, bird song, food, a good run, connecting with someone. Interestingly too, it is rarely 'stuff' that makes me happy or at least, happiest. I can count on one hand the number of times that I have written about an item or object in my gratitude journal, yet I am drawn to clothes / shoes / household stuff like a moth to a flame! That's something I want to change and work on in the next 12 months.

Resilience – probably one of the top 10 words of the pandemic and would definitely feature in a game of covid bingo! This last year has shown me how resilient we can all be. Myself included. From businesses adapting to produce a new product or service, the brilliant response of the NHS, teachers creating remote learning resources, and parents and carers overseeing that learning. The list could go on, it has been inspiring and reassuring to see how adaptable we can all be when really needed.

Closer to home, I've worried about my boys and how they would cope being isolated from friends, finding the motivation to do their schoolwork, and missing out on months of swimming and football training. I needn't have worried, they have just got on with it, mostly smiling, mostly taking each day as it comes and finding new and different ways to create enjoyment and fun. Each time lockdown has eased, they simply picked back up where they left off and always with a smile!

Kindness – we have witnessed some amazing, heart-warming stories of acts of kindness. There have been the big stories reported on national news as well as those closer to home, the businesses who helped deliver food parcels, the closed restaurants who cooked for the homeless, and the neighbours who looked out for the vulnerable on their street. I hope that sense of community, those acts of kindness don't fade away as we move out of the storm of the pandemic and back towards a less turbulent way of living. It has been wonderful to talk to my children about kindness and seeing the good in people and using these examples to counter the inevitable 'less kind' actions and sentiments that have also taken place during the last year.

Connections – loneliness has been one of the awful consequences of the pandemic, we can all feel lonely at times, even when we live with a house full of people! Flicking through my gratitude diary I noticed that connecting and connection feature a lot. My days have been lifted by a phone call with a colleague, a joke over a Zoom meeting, or a message or call to a friend.

I read recently, that one of the reasons people have supported shopping locally is that they have enjoyed the connections with shop staff. I would totally agree, sometimes a smile, "hello, how are you?" at the till is enough to lift my spirits, and my boys are always rather embarrassed when I wave enthusiastically at people we pass in the street!

Science – I am no scientist, despite harbouring a desire to be a surgeon at the tender age of 9! I gave up physics as soon as I could, and I delegate all non-arithmetic related school maths to my husband. Perhaps it is because I don't exercise the scientific part of my brain that I have developed such respect, admiration and awe for the scientists that have been guiding us through this last year and in particular to those developing the vaccinations. I am a fully signed up Radio 4 listener and other regular listeners will know that they tend to call in the same handful of scientists to explain an issue. Consequently, I have a group of favourites for whom the volume is turned up, the children hushed, and their wise words stored and repeated in those doom and gloom moments. Their calmness and considered explanations based predominantly on fact, have kept me going and given me hope and comfort. For me, they are amongst the heroes of the pandemic and I hope that they have inspired children and young people to consider a career in science.

Hope – I use the word hope a lot, mainly to open an email or letter, "I hope you are well…" etc. It is only in these last few months that I have fully appreciated those four letters, their power and strength. I am now a fully paid-up member of the Hope fan club. I didn't 'get' hope until the end of 2020, I didn't feel it, I couldn't see or touch it. I knew we were heading for another lockdown but when it came on Christmas Eve it broke me. It was a radio interview sometime between Christmas and New Year with the CEO of Astra Zeneca and the Oxford University lead Professor that got through to me. The combination of the second vaccine to be approved within the year, plus the not-for profit- greater-good approach, sparked hope.

I've no doubt that the year ahead will be challenging, and, when it gets tough, these six things will help me get through.

Friday 9th April 2021: DW
Are we there yet?

Some questions are more difficult than others, eh?

And don't worry this isn't a quiz.

A couple of weeks before Michelle mentioned that she was going to ask those who initially wrote for this collective diary last year to write a further piece a year later, I read about the concept of the 'provisional life'. The Swiss psychologist Marie-Louise von Franz explained it as "a strange feeling that one is *not yet* in real life. For the time being, one is doing this or that… [but] there is always the fantasy that sometime in the future the real thing will come about."

Back in March of last year when everything suddenly changed, the provisional life was something that was forced upon us all regardless of whether we were happy to accept it or not. Everything became framed against the suggestion that when all of this was over, we could get back to normal. However, as time passed it became clear that this temporary existence was one that we'd be living in for longer than we would have hoped, and to a greater or lesser extent was now a normal that we were perhaps reluctant to accept.

With that being the case, it has inevitably been a year of learning, with every day a school day. And for me, the main lesson has been understanding that whatever situation I find myself in the best way forward is to adapt to it and carry on regardless, rather than hoping that "sometime in the future the real thing will come about". Quite why it has taken me so long to learn this fairly straightforward lesson is not something that I'm going to spend any time worrying about, and whether I'll be able to put that learning into action is another matter entirely – maybe ask me again in April 2022.

I started my initial entry with a somewhat modified quote (sorry John) from the very beginning of my favourite post-apocalyptic novel, The Day of the Triffids by John Wyndham.

So, having inevitably looked back at that ahead of writing this it seemed appropriate to finish with a further quote from the same book, but this time from the very end. Because while we haven't been driving back "predatory plants which are capable of growing to a gigantic size and are possessed of locomotive ability and a poisonous sting" it has sometimes felt like we may as well have been.

Saturday 10th April 2021: Michal Siewniak
When it all began

It was Saturday, 28 March 2020. I remember it well. It was, at least for us in the UK, the first full week in the lockdown. It felt strange and unreal. At times, it felt like I was watching a science fiction movie. Towns deserted, very few people out, notices everywhere that only a handful of people is allowed in to shop. Panic buying as if it was the end of the world. I had been asking myself, maybe it is the end on the world as we know it?

Deaths, people losing jobs, companies closing down, anxiety levels (for a number of reasons) are going through the roof. Imposed isolation and loneliness of the most vulnerable members of our community and our fantastic NHS stretched to the absolute limits. The list was long, wasn't it? Covid-19 didn't and still doesn't recognise any barriers, borders, and treats everyone 'equally'. It affects us all and there are very few, if any, spots on the planet where we could go and feel safe. One virus, complete standstill. Simply staggering.

For me, the lockdown started on Friday night, 20 March 2020, when I came back late from work and I went straight to my local church to attend our last public Mass before the quarantine began. It was such a profound moment. Total and complete silence, no hand shaking, no sign of peace. It felt different and yet so beautiful. I felt deep unity and hope that God is with us, especially now when we, globally and in our local communities, were so badly affected by this crisis.

The next morning, I went to my local pharmacy. My town, Welwyn Garden City, looked so empty. The same Saturday, 21 March 2020, I helped to organise a very quick 'social action'. I suggested to the Polish community in Welwyn Hatfield to support, in a practical way, one of the local charities. After a quick conversation with Welwyn Hatfield Community Voluntary Services, I rang Welwyn Hatfield Women's Refuge.

This short phone call was quite emotional. I knew that our simple 'act of generosity' would help residents who found themselves in exceptionally difficult circumstances. In order to obey social distancing, we drove in three separate cars, most people who were donating food left everything on their doorsteps. All organised in 36 hours. What a relief and joy!

My learning during the first month of the lockdown
One phrase which particularly struck with me at the beginning, and which I am still learning to implement, was to 'count your blessings'. Being at home 24/7 took a bit of time to get used to, it had its big challenges however, I also started noticing some advantages: a simple picnic in the garden seemed like a great social outing. Reading or colouring in the garden probably can't replace a classroom however it was good to see that actual learning never stops and it could take place in any location! My youngest daughter, who is six, while in the lockdown, wrote me her first letter. I decided, for obvious reasons, not to take her for our infrequent shopping. When I returned, she gave me a piece of paper which said: "To Dad, you made Eva sad". It was heart-breaking but I was delighted that her letter had no spelling mistakes! Having a garden is a luxury! It must be a lot harder when you are stuck at home and your movement is limited.

Some learning during the first lockdown
I must admit that I actually enjoyed the first lockdown. There was no need to take kids to school, no need to travel and generally there was no morning rush. I was glad that for once, I didn't have to be in various places at the same time. It was also good to stay at home, simply 'be' with the family in the present moment. I also had, maybe for the first time, more time look after myself.

However, it was true that the Covid-19 experience of the lockdown was and is an emotional rollercoaster. I often felt like a 'bird who can't fly'. It felt like my movements and freedom were hugely limited. The routine, being, living, relaxing, and working in the same place was actually tiring. Zoom meetings were becoming more difficult. It was not always easy to listen and read the body language, especially if I was in a meeting with many other people. I missed the office environment, I missed opportunities for real 'human interactions'.

Easter, which last year happened during the lockdown, was so special. No ability to go to church, no physical presence in our places of worship and yet, the whole Easter period has been such an enriching experience. Taking part in online church services was profound and comforting. In the last four-six months, I have visited churches in Belfast, Glasgow, and Limerick. I have been travelling a lot, online!

Work-life balance during the Covid-19 crisis
Working from home has a lot of advantages. The current pandemic has, even if for not for all of us, slowed things down. We are/were stuck indoors with a very limited ability to go out. For me, one of the greatest lessons during the health pandemic is the recognition that the work-life balance is essential in keeping us healthy. Our body needs to 'recharge its batteries' and it is so important for each one of us to know when to take a break. Yep, our head does need a space!

During the lockdown, I have also realised (yes, it took me 40 years!) that life is not always a sprint but more often a marathon and we need to know when to slow down and when to move a bit faster. In October 2013, a friend of mine, who I was helping to run a health MOT event, checked my blood pressure. It was high. It is ok now, however I had to start taking medication. What she said to me then will stay with me forever. We need to listen to our body. So simple and so hard to do, at least for me.

Opportunities for dialogue
Dalai Lama once said: *"When you talk, you are only repeating what you already know; but when you listen, you learn something new."*

One of the best parts of the lockdown were my daily evening walks with my Polish male friends. They truly were a fantastic discovery. It is not often easy for guys to open up, however the longer we talk and the longer I actively listened, the more fruitful our dialogue became. Each one of us needed sometimes a 'friendly listening ear'. An opportunity to be for the other person can make a huge difference. My part in all of it? Not much. It is often more important to simply 'be' in that moment with this person. Such a simple thing to say and not always easy to implement in our daily routines. During the lockdown, I have understood that active listening is a skill which we all should try and develop. It is crucial to enhance our relationships. During my daily evening walks, I had a chance to help a friend, who was struggling mentally and whose marriage was going through a crisis.

Discovering new talents during the national lockdowns
I have a master's degree in history, however for the last 12 years, I have been working in the charity sector. Why? I am an activist by nature. I am a 'doer', I like 'doing stuff' and I initially thought that I would struggle during all three lockdowns as our opportunities to e.g. run events, organise and set up community initiatives have been limited or, in many cases, impossible.

However, lockdown helped me to discover that I really enjoy writing! There are a number of subjects, which are close to my heart including: diversity, migration, faith, dialogue, civic engagement, or the rights of the EU nationals. I am absolutely delighted that, since September 2020, I wrote 20+ articles for Polonia24, a Polish online portal in the UK. On Monday 29th March, I was also absolutely delighted to receive an email from the Deputy Editor of my local paper, Welwyn Hatfield Times. I was asked to write a monthly column for the Polish community. I am rather pleased that so called 'hard to reach groups' (or easy to ignore!) will have an opportunity to shape local news and that the paper itself is keen to encourage local residents to take an active role in making news more inclusive and accessible! My question is: could this be my next career move?

Conclusion:
In my case, the last year 13 months helped me hugely to look at my life priorities (still an ongoing process!), re-evaluate what it is that I want to do, and although I have not fully discovered what the future will bring, I remain hopeful and optimistic.

Do I still worry? Of course. The current health pandemic is something we all, individually and collectively, have not experienced before. The fear of unknown and the unpredictability of our future means that we feel lost. There is still a long way to go, however we must remain faithful and hope that we will get through this crisis together. I hope that this difficult and challenging chapter in our history will help us to build a sense of real family, global family which accepts each member with open arms and a big heart. Our journey continues and I know that despite huge sacrifices and suffering, we will go through this crisis.

Sunday 11th April 2021: Abbie Panks
Been a bit weird hasn't it?

When I first wrote my reflections last year, I headed into lockdown life thinking that we would be in for a few months of a quieter life before normality would return, I was very wrong on both fronts!

I, like many others, spent hours a day watching the news and reading papers, trying to absorb as much information as I could about this strange new world we were living in. It was exhausting and soon enough information overload hit, and If I'm totally honest, it started to scare me a bit.

Eventually, I stopped the obsessive news watching and for the first time in a very, very long time, took a digital detox to try and ease my worried mind.

The phrase *'go where you are needed'* often circulates around in my brain and so that, along with my inability to sit still for long, meant I decided to try and make myself useful.

Quite early on it became apparent that there were lots of people in the immediate and wider community who needed support, so I threw myself into doing as much as I could on that front, both for individuals who needed help with shopping, gardening or errands running but also community ventures, charities and businesses who needed support with changes required to help them continue to trade and grow in this new Covid-driven world. It's been heartening to see how innovative people have been, not just with their businesses but coming up with solutions to support their communities during a time of intense challenges.

Just before Christmas, a chance meeting in my village with a NHS worker led to me stepping forward to help coordinate the volunteer effort for the vaccination rollout in west Norfolk - if it wasn't for the NHS, I wouldn't be here now. They've saved me in the past and they've been under so much pressure over the last year, supporting them felt like lifting a small bit of the weight from their shoulders, and the very least I could do.

Six months in and thousands have been vaccinated and its genuinely such a happy environment to be in. In addition to the clinical team, I've been working with a team of 80 amazing volunteers. I've learnt volunteering is a two-way thing. Not only are the clinical team happy for the help, the patients are also really happy to see you there helping deliver vaccinations. For the volunteers, it also gives an enormous boost of wellbeing. I spoke to another over tea break one day who told me how the volunteering had saved her, and that it had given her a real feeling of purpose. Another told me how it was the only human interaction he had had. Both statements had quite a profound effect on me.

Aside from that, I've not learnt any new skills (crumpet making aside) or picked up any more hobbies, I've not gotten fit and lost weight (quite the opposite, sadly, see previous crumpet point) but I do feel like I've gotten to know myself better, I have learnt that I enjoy simple pleasures a lot more than I realised, and how much I like people, even grumpy ones

In 'real life' a huge part of everything I do workwise is about bringing people together, and I've really, REALLY missed that. Whether that's bringing them into a leisure space, or to an event or into a business – it's all ultimately about connection and that's been one of the most challenging things to work around during the pandemic. The lack of social connection has been challenging but it feels like we now have a unique opportunity to create a new future where people and our communities are our priority.

Monday 12th April 2021: Helen Hooper

2020 - what a year, right? The best and the worst all rolled into one. Filled with disappointment, loss, excitement, and the realisation of an internal power I didn't know I possessed.

Those first days and weeks were tough and I quickly realised that I needed to turn to the one thing that has always soothed and sustained me - my fitness. I have always had a passion for health and exercise, but the truth was that at the start of lockdown I was burnt out and had definitely lost my mojo.

Time had been my enemy but now I had all the time in the world and it was exactly what I needed. I thrive on situations that push me and so I used my time wisely. Physically and mentally I now feel stronger than I have ever done, which held me in good stead to deal with the loss that was thrown at us later in the year.

My best friend and I have known each other since we were seven and as a result our mums became extremely close too. Both were very ill last year (non-covid related) and in November, in the space of a week, we lost them both. We think they may have hatched a pact at some point in time over a glass of wine!

Mum was a beautiful person and her loss is something that I feel every day. But she is such an inspiration to me. She was always smiling, always thinking of others, and I strive to be like her.

My love of animals definitely comes from her. Back in July I saw a picture of a little cat living in Greece and being looked after by a sanctuary I support. She had no nose due to cancer, was suffering from FIV, and had been abandoned when she was really poorly and needed help the most.

I immediately knew she was my cat and I contacted the charity to say I wanted to adopt her. Long months followed as she recovered enough to travel and waiting for all the relevant lockdowns in the three countries involved in her journey lifted.

The law of attraction is something that I work on in my life, and I decided to let the universe work out all the necessary logistics of getting Bella to us. I put a picture of her up on the wall so I saw her every day and was in constant contact with the sanctuary. It worked.

To say her arrival with us was cut to the wire would be an understatement. I finally drove to collect her from the personal escort that she had (someone from the sanctuary literally travelled with her all the way from Greece) in mid-December. In fact it was just three days before the UK and France shut their borders to each other. I believe Mum may have had a hand in getting her to us!

Bella had been travelling for three days and yet she walked out of her cat basket into our kitchen like the little sass she is. From the moment she arrived she has lapped up all the love we have given her like a sponge, and still comes back for more. It's like she is making up for all the lost time she had when she had been abandoned and treated badly.

What a lesson in living in the moment, and what a way to end the year!

So what am I taking from 2020 and moving forward with?

Well, life is life. It's up and it's down and you can't predict any of it. You can choose to curl up and hide away when it gets too scary, or you can stand up, look it in the face and surf that wave.

Things may not look as we had planned them, but the trouble with planning the future is that you forget to live the present.

It's not a mistake I intend to make again.

I am moving forward with fresh intention to enjoy every day for what it gives. No more and no less.

Tuesday 13th April 2021: Tom Page
Has a year gone by already?

This time twelve months ago we all started to experience something that hitherto I thought only happened in other places.

I remember the first SARS outbreak in China in 2002 and more recently the Ebola outbreak in West Africa in 2014. Both epidemics spurred governments into action, and I remember thanking whoever we say thanks to that these horrors were not being visited upon us.

All that changed in 2020 and looking back I can see that even as we locked down, I did not understand quite what we were in for. I remember saying things like "see you on the other side" suggesting that we would lockdown for a few weeks and then the virus would go away. I was wrong.

During the first lockdown we all went in with a sort of comradery; Joe Wicks did his workouts while the rest of us Zoom called and did pub quizzes in front of laptops. That "see you on the other side" spirit was present in not just me.

This latest lockdown, for me, did not have those qualities; this was not new, not novel, and not fun. Completely necessary though it was, it robbed me of the last of my innocence when it came to this virus. Maybe that is not such a bad thing, but morale took a dip.

I look back on the last year with a sense of gratitude. Not for the pandemic but for what I have that has sustained me through this most turbulent of years.

I am grateful for my family and the fact they are close, I am grateful for my friends and colleagues who have kept morale up, grateful that I have been able to work from home keeping safe, and grateful for my home itself.

I am grateful to all key workers who have remained on the front lines of this pandemic all year and I am grateful to the scientists who are our only hope of defeating this virus.

This pandemic has held a mirror up to society and I weep when I think of the conditions that others have had to endure through this pandemic.

This experience has changed my outlook and will permanently change my behaviour. For instance, in years to come if I am feeling unwell, I will wear a mask in the supermarket and I will not martyr myself at my desk at work if I am ill.

I can also see that whilst working from home I am able to resist the litany of distractions that home provides and more importantly I can resist opening the fridge too often.

As we emerge from this lockdown I think of the future. My immediate concern is to be vaccinated so I can hug my mum again, have a pint in the pub with friends, and maybe take a train trip somewhere as I have not left King's Lynn for fourteen months and counting.

Longer term I am going to make far more effort to see friends and family far more often than before. Those opportunities can be taken away and I will not take them for granted as I really missed seeing people over the last few months.

Let us all hope this lockdown will be the last and our amazing NHS continues their remarkable vaccine rollout. Things will not go back to normal any time soon, but my hope is that we can have a steady march towards normality with tangible progress that we can all feel.

Wednesday 14 April 2021: Chris Playford
Well, with lockdown coming to an end after these long winter months, it's certainly been a very different experience, but in other ways it's been much the same as always. Whereas I used to get my kicks from going off to some hot and steamy faraway place, I now get them tending to my carefully nurtured veggie plants or watching the male pheasants in the garden fighting over the females. Whatever the case, the constant ups and the downs of my mood still follow the same patterns as always, so in my head not that much has changed. All that said, I do concur that lockdown has been extremely tedious, but I must also add how very fortunate we are living here in rural mid-Norfolk and being able to step out of our back door to walk or cycle in the glorious countryside which is so peaceful and mostly empty.

Anyway, just a few weeks ago I had my Covid jab. I got the Oxford one, no side effects for me but Sue, who I live with, had 24 hours of the shivers and headaches. After the three weeks' wait for it to take efficacy, I am now bursting with energy and ready to get on with things. HM Government have stated that after only one jab we are 80% less likely of contracting serious illness or dying. So based on this information being correct, rightly or wrongly I feel armour coated and am ready to resume normal life.

On the matter of the vaccine, a few of my friends are not going to have it, based on a number of worries and concerns about side effects as well as some more outlandish conspiracy theories. One of my long-time friends, who's nearly eighty with a few health issues, is adamant he is not having it. I know there has been some criticism of those people who choose not to get vaccinated, with accusations of them not playing their part or being selfish in the concerted effort to overcome this virus. I don't necessarily agree with this view, I believe it should and must remain a fundamental human right as to what we choose to ingest into our body, including (alcohol, fags, chocolate, etc.). So, the decision to have or not have the vaccine must remain a free one.

We (Sue and I) were in a similar situation in regard to getting infected with malaria whilst working in Sierra Leone. Malaria is caught through mosquito bites and is endemic in Sierra Leone, it poses a constant threat, as a result you are strongly advised to take prophylactics by the medical fraternity. As with the covid jab taking malaria prophylactics does not necessarily prevent you getting the disease but greatly reduces the likelihood of serious illness or death. Consequently, there was always great debate, mainly among the expat community in regard to taking or not taking malaria prophylactics, and again like the Covid jab there was some outlandish predictions as to what might happen to your body if taken on a long-term basis. So, the issues in taking malaria prophylactics and having the Covid jab revolve around the same worries and concerns. On the malaria front It worked out like this for us: Sue took the prophylactics all of the time and never got malaria. I, on the other hand, did not always take it and suffice to say I got malaria. So, I guess it is this experience as much as anything which has influenced us both to have the jab. It seems it has become the great debate of 2021: to get Covid jabbed or not to get jabbed.

Back to the lockdown. As already said a million times, by so many, the lockdown has been a trial of patience and I like so many others have sorely missed seeing my family, chasing my lovely grandkids round the garden, hugging and spending time with my daughters as well as dropping in to see old mates for a chat. Also, my dear old dad died last summer during the restrictions (not from Covid) and like many others we had a restricted funeral, and not being able to have a proper wake for him was a real bummer.

On a lighter note, not being able to go to the pub has been a constant miss and unfortunately drinking at home has at times registered on the addiction graph! Not been able to go to

Carrow Road to watch live football has also been a miss, especially as the Canaries have been virtually invincible this season. So nurturing plants from seeds to edible beautiful vegetables, going for walks, and watching the birds has been my solace.

So, at last life is returning to some form of normality and this coming week is awesome, which has not always been the case during the long winter lockdown when some weeks the only exciting thing that happened was when the bins were collected on a Thursday.

So, for this week:
- Monday: the pubs are opening! The shops are opening! We can get a haircut! We can meet our friends and family outside! Boris has deemed it so!
- Tuesday: I'm back in the garden planting my sweet pea plants.
- Wednesday is huge, our local pub (The Earle Arms, Heydon) opens for the first time in months. I fitted a new toilet in the Ladies a few weeks ago, so I'm hoping for preferential service during the clamour for beer at the bar.
- Thursday: it's horse manure carting, and of course its bin day!
- Friday: after all that excitement I will need to take it easy and will probably have a kip in the afternoon in anticipation of super Saturday.
- Saturday: it's immense. Not only will I see my sister and brother for the first time since last year for a meet up on the North Norfolk coast but to finish the week off in the evening Norwich City play Bournemouth and if they win, we are promoted to the premier league. What a perfect finish to the lockdown! Let's have a party!

Hope everyone enjoys the long-awaited release from lockdown.

Thursday 15th April 2021: Emma O'Shaughnessy

It feels significant to me to sit down and reflect today. I dropped the kids off at school for what I hope is their first interrupted term for over a year and went straight out for a 60-minute walk on my own by design. I then bumped into some friends at the end which was lovely and so could tick my favourite box - the best of both! I went straight to my first hair appointment since December and in the middle of it got a picture message from my husband who had received a last-minute call from the vaccination centre and had the jab 20 minutes later. Not only that but he gets in his second in four weeks' time. In four weeks' time we'll be a fully vaccinated household. I was speechless.

Literally nothing happened for months and by 10.43 everything had happened! Sod's law but I'm not complaining. It did feel like a new chapter when I got up first thing but life has a way of reinforcing things – today was a good day for us!

I don't tend to look back, even when I do I intuitively look for the positive of the past 12 months. For me, personally, it has been the simple things. The time we all have had together, the things we have learnt about each other and ourselves as our small unit of four. The renewed love of exercise that has got all of us through, the kitten, the new food we introduced the kids to, the walks I doubt we would ever have found had it not been for lockdown.

When I take my rose-tinted glasses off, it was tough. I'm new to freelance life and the pandemic took its toll. Things are looking better now but I'm 12 months behind where I should be and that's a worry. Yet despite the challenges professionally as I'm re-emerging, work is probably my most significant reflection. All the work I'm involved in is as a direct result of the pandemic. Either because of circumstance or because Covid has changed our working worlds immensely. It's quality work, striving to give more purpose and set organisations up for long term sustainable change and it's the most engaged I have been for a long time. It's not just me, I'm having many, many conversations with all sorts of people whose working lives have been changed by the pandemic and they are thriving in more purposeful roles, looking for ways to keep it going as things get back to normal.

My other significant reflection is my crew. I strongly believe the people in our social groups and our networks who sustained us through these months will forever be in our lives. Our families, those we missed the most and those drive-bys or doorstep drops when we could see but not touch – so alien, but I'll never forget how joyful and how hard they were. Those people we worked with, whose pets we came to know, whose bedrooms we Zoomed in to day in day out, whose partners we met through delivery of the odd cuppa will find they are the team that we remember for years to come. The old school friendship groups reenergised, and the comfort of re-connecting with old friends and for me the school mums – still my newest bunch but God did they get me through it – each one of us different but joined together by community and a common bond of home schooling. It feels like our friendship has been deepened not by the virtue of many years but the intensity of such extreme times.

One day we'll be sitting in a pub garden and we'll say, *"do you remember that year?"* That year with no school, working from home, no holidays and it will feel so alien. I strongly believe that if we can follow it up with a few *"and look what wouldn't be true now if it wasn't for Covid"* then we'll have grown. God knows for those people we have all lost through the past year we owe it to them to take richness from the experience and never let it go.

Friday 16th April 2021: Helen Terry

The Cambridge Half Marathon – 8th March 2020. That's my last memory of 'normal life'. I did a personal best and felt pretty epic. But even then we were starting to get a bit twitchy. A Cambridge professor was lobbying for the race to be cancelled (quite rightly, in retrospect) and when the guy on the breakfast table next to me at the B&B coughed in my direction, I remember feeling extremely anxious and giving him the side-eye. My Cambridge Half Marathon memento was a hessian shopping bag. Every single time I take it to the shops, as I will do in a moment, it reminds me of a pre-Covid world.

Cambridge onwards seems a bit of a blur. I remember feeling that you should "be careful what you wish for". I went from being an extremely time-poor freelancer, wishing I could spend more time with my daughter and feeling constantly guilty, to all my work drying up and suddenly becoming a teacher and full-time playmate and spending every waking hour of my day with her. It was so tough at times, especially in the second wave when we didn't have that glorious weather. But I got to spend that time with her and becoming such a fundamental part of her learning felt like a huge achievement.

I've never been so frightened as I have been in the last year though. Three of my daughter's four grandparents ended up in hospital with serious (non-Covid) conditions. Communication was poor. I thought I was going to lose my mum at one point and not being able to be with her and hold her hand was both terrifying and heart-breaking.

That was the worst part – the extra layer of fear and complexity to the rest of the things that life inevitably throws at you, such as when three of my beautiful friends were diagnosed with cancer – two having mastectomies and one starting chemotherapy. And, heartbreakingly, my friend losing her seven-year-old niece to DIPG. Covid has made everything even more complicated and harder for them and their families.

The most positive things have been the strengthening of relationships. My husband deserves a medal for being such a rock – bringing the money in, peeling me off the floor when my mood and strength plummeted and stepping in when he could feel home-schooling tensions rising. After 14 years of marriage, if nothing else, 2020 confirmed that he was the guy for me. I'm not 100% sure if it's reciprocated after all I've thrown at him, but he's still here!

We're extremely lucky to get on well with all our parents and lucky that they also get on well with each other. As a unit we've been there for each other, with weekly 'Friday wine time Zooms' and group chats. Even though it wasn't what we hoped for, we got our Christmas together. It gave us the boost we all needed to get us through the next few months as Covid once again tore through our communities.

And then there are my amazing friends. I am lucky to have several individuals and pockets of friends who have just been incredible. Supporting each other, gifts, pick-me-ups, long chats, socially distanced runs, and dog walks… and the brilliant gifs and memes. I simply do not know what I would have done without them.

My running club, Norfolk Gazelles, has also been phenomenal. Virtual challenges, fantastic virtual training sessions and staging a virtual relay event last May which was less about speed and more about who could run with the most ridiculous baton. Running up University Drive with men's captain Lee wearing a washing machine as his baton will never cease to make me smile.

I think the thing that has amazed me the most is the resilience of the people around me. But none more so than my little girl, who swiftly accepted "because of the virus" as an answer to 99% of her questions and who 'just got on with it'. She coped with it all so much better than I expected and maintained a pretty positive attitude throughout. She was so lonely, but she's bounced back. What a little star.

Just before Christmas I felt I'd completely lost all sense of who I was. I had a really black period and I think it's the closest I've come to depression. But I'm now clawing it back. The work is starting to come in again and I'm volunteering on an amazing initiative with The Outdoor Guide Foundation to get outdoor gear to kids who need it the most in primary schools. If nothing else, I hope the pandemic has created a new generation of nature-loving adventure-seekers.

I feel I'll always be closer to tears than I was before March 2020. I've learnt so much about myself and the attitudes of others. But I want to channel the strong emotions into something positive, so I'm going to run my little socks off on my birthday at the London Marathon this year and raise money for the charities that have supported my friends.

Today, 16th April 2021, I'm reflecting on the sheer excitement of where that Cambridge Half Marathon bag can go compared to a year ago. The gratitude for the little things will never leave me. Every little easing of the restrictions brings a little bit more joy and I'm reacquainting myself with the positive outlook I've been so desperate to find in recent months. Hopefully I can finally see my brother and his family who live abroad again soon.

The bag is a strong and sturdy thing – it's carried some pretty hefty loads (including much wine) and it will go on for years. So as well as a reminder of the past, I think I'll use it as a symbol of strength going forwards. That whatever load we carry, we're strong enough to get through it, even though we don't think we are.

Saturday 17th April 2021: Donna-Louise Bishop
Lockdown Survival 101: How to get through a pandemic

I own you an apology. This title is misleading. After spending a year in some form or another of lockdown, quite frankly I have no idea how to survive one.

It's a badass title though, right?

Maybe I'm not giving myself enough credit here. I'll start at the beginning.

Before March 2020, I was a part-time working mum to three young boys, aged seven, five, and two, and dating a wonderful man called Allan. More than a year on, I remain a part-time working mum to three young boys, who are now aged eight, six, and three, and we are now *living* with a wonderful man called Allan (who now also happens to be my fiancé as of 22 May, 2021).

Talk about a baptism of fire, but we decided to take a leap into the world of blended/extended/step/co-habiting (whatever it's called these days) family life just days before the official lockdown began.

Don't get me wrong, plans had been in the pipeline, but the plans were moved up a little quicker than perhaps I'd been ready for. You know what, though? I think we've done ourselves proud.

During the first month there may have been a few incidents of bickering and generally getting on each other's nerves, but with the pubs being shut there was just no safe haven to ship him off too. Five people. One house. A tiny garden. And too many emotions to count. That's basically been us for 12 months.

One day though, when I was finally able to grab ten minutes with a hot (yes, hot!) cup of tea, I sat back and smiled at the little and new home we'd built around ourselves. I was sitting on a sofa Allan had brought with him from his flat, looking at a kitchen installed before his arrival but one we had colour-schemed together, while listening to him explain patiently to the boys for the millionth time how to put their clothes away (not the youngest one, mind you – he was probably hiding somewhere in the house causing a mischief).

Although we were trapped in our own little kingdom, we were building up our castle one brick at a time.

I've always enjoyed spending time alone in the house, sometimes counting down the minutes till the boys went to bed and I could enjoy wine-o-clock by myself watching Teen Mom UK (don't judge). Now I had a real-life actual adult there in the evenings. What was I meant to do to keep him entertained?

I found out quickly that a loving relationship doesn't have to always be about the grand gestures. And the bond between parent and child isn't created by spending money on them.

So, what *did* we do?

We enjoyed eating cheese and biscuits delivered from a local cheesemonger, movie nights devouring bowls and bowls of popcorn, baking, baking, and baking, reading books to chill us out, playing silly games on the Kindle to make us laugh, watching the kids create thousands of pieces of art work, sneaking the thousands of pieces of art work into the recycling bin, celebrating birthdays, watching music videos and dancing along to them, getting knackered doing Joe Wicks then deciding to do Cosmic Kids yoga instead because it was so much easier, home schooling, more home schooling, then not so much home schooling as there were too many tears, and finally lots and lots and lots and LOTS of walks with homemade nature trails provided by me.

If I didn't know my local village before, I certainly do now; every nook, cranny, corner, and unturned stone.

Looking back, I would describe the time spent in lockdown worrying and stressful. Yet, I can't help but remember all the good times more so than the bad.

My boys have grown to love the new adult in their lives, and in return he has grown to love them as his own. We feel like a family. Heck, we *are* a family. We've had the opportunity to get to know each other better, which living under the same roof has a way of doing.

I'm not going to lie and say the extra time spent with my family was all sprinkles and rainbows – I like going to work and I like hearing about my children's day at school - because time together and quality time together are two different things. But it has still been time worthwhile and a time which I will cherish as a year of new beginnings.

The knock-on effects are of course ones that are on par with so many others. Although I have not lost someone I love to Covid, I have written many obituaries and tribute pieces for the paper I work for of people who have. I have also joined far too many others on the road to overcoming mental illness (thanks Doc for the tablets, and the bi-weekly counselling). And I am completely, entirely, categorically over the phrases socially-distanced, the new normal, tier systems, as well as always forgetting to take a mask with me!

So, if you really want to know how to survive lockdown in a pandemic, I'd suggest not taking my advice but the advice from one of my boys' favourite cartoons, Apple and Onion, which in my house has been watched only a few million times during lockdown: "Take it one step at a time and you'll find your way."

Oh, and save the chocolate biscuits for emergencies only. Have an apple instead – your post-lockdown body will thank you.

Sunday 18th April 2021: Ronda Jackson

Normal life seems like a lifetime ago. I am not even sure I can remember what normal was anymore. I guess we have all adapted to our new normal.

I am (was) a single mum with two children aged 2 and 12 and I run a debt recovery business working full time.

I had my hands full before lockdown and I certainly had my hands full during lockdown.

Being a business owner and a sole provider for my children I was definitely nervous initially about what would happen to my job, my income, and the economy during the lockdown period. Thankfully, I am one of the lucky ones that have managed to carry on working throughout the pandemic. I am so grateful for that.

It did mean the office came to my home and my meetings went onto Zoom and I now spend hardly anything on petrol for the car anymore.

Me and my girls went on many walks around the village doing more than one a day on the days when we could.

Thankfully, this meant I met the love of my life down the local shop. He also lived in the village and we managed to form a relationship during lockdown. Seems crazy to think this man lived less than a mile from my home and I had never met him or seen him before in my life. If it wasn't for lockdown and my endless walks around the village we may never have met.

I still feel like we have done dating in reverse as we still haven't really managed to go for meals out or even go to the cinema together or have drinks in a bar.

Our first official date was in his garden.

Some days have been hard trying to work and home-school and having two children at home. I have often had to rely on my 12-year-old to supervise my 2-year-old while I am working. I also felt like many people were craving seeing people when I found myself sometimes craving some time alone.

During the various ups and downs of the lockdown the second lockdown for me was by far the hardest. My eldest daughter was taken into hospital for most of November which was a scary time.

Luckily with her only being twelve I was able to be with her in hospital but I got to see the inside of a hospital during a global pandemic and it was a completely different environment.

The hospital was empty. No visitors I mean. Even children were only allowed one parent present. We had to be Covid tested before we were moved to the ward and once on the ward, they really encouraged you to stay where you were.

This meant I spent a lot of time away from my youngest daughter which was really hard too. It was hard not having family around me to be able to support me.

It's quite worrying when in hospital and you need desperate help for your child and you realise how stretched the services are.

Thankfully we were out of hospital for Christmas. Christmas was a little different too as I could not be with my entire family as I had wished. Everyone had a present which I could order from Amazon as Christmas shopping was just never going to happen. Fortunately we did see this coming so my family had a fake Christmas in October when the restrictions were lifted slightly.

With the weather being dark and cold it felt even harder to drag myself out for a walk. The days felt long and I often had that 'I need a holiday' feeling.

We have turned a corner and the future looks brighter. My parents and now my sister have received the first vaccine. I am hoping to get mine shortly. I think this will all help us look for a brighter future.

On reflection I am still so grateful for all the time I have been able to spend with my children. We have enjoyed some real good quality time together and those memories I will cherish forever.

Monday 19th April 2021: Stephanie Brighton

Monday March 16th 2020 might not have seemed like a significant date for 2020 but for me it was. It was the last day I taught children face to face. School was starting to change and we had begun making restrictions to visitors, parents, and how we were teaching. I had left for work that day expecting to return, albeit knowing that things were changing daily. That evening I had attended my running club and returned home to see my husband looking very concerned. Whilst I was out they had announced the 'vulnerable' groups, those they suggested worked from home and took greater care in avoiding Covid-19. Pregnant women were on the list. I was on the list.... 10 weeks pregnant with our rainbow baby - we both quickly became terribly anxious.

I contacted my head teacher immediately and was reassured that I could start working from home. I was told not to come into work to protect myself and my baby. I spent the rest of the week videoing stories, activities, and lessons for my year group, hoping they'd be useful. The week continued with more news emerging and in particular that schools were to 'close' to all except those children of key workers. On the Friday I took my son to school and briefly spoke to his teacher (from a distance of course). We both spoke with a wobble in our voices, worried for the uncertain weeks ahead.

It was tricky being at home when I hadn't announced my pregnancy. Close friends knew but the majority didn't. However, being an asthmatic too I could say to most that I was off due to being in the vulnerable group of those with asthma.

As the weeks went on I'd like to say the anxiety eased but it didn't. Although we had been for an early scan at eight weeks I was still so worried this baby would not make it. It's probably at this point I should explain. In 2015 I gave birth to our first son. The pregnancy was smooth, even though the birth wasn't.

In 2017 I lost a baby at approximately seven weeks. It was my first miscarriage. A year later in 2018 I had what is called a 'missed miscarriage'. Two consecutive miscarriages, so you can see why I was so anxious with this pregnancy. My 12-week scan was due in April just as restrictions were tightening, therefore, my husband couldn't attend. I understood why and accepted this but it didn't make it any easier. I sat in the waiting area and cried, scared for what I would see on the screen this time and avoiding all eye contact from others. Thankfully, a beautiful thriving baby was wiggling away. I cried with relief and couldn't wait to put my husband's mind at ease too. This was also the day we told our son he was having a much longed for sibling.

Pregnancy in lockdown was tough. Managing home schooling as well as my own job as a teacher and being exhausted was not an ideal scenario to say the least! I constantly felt worried. Worried that I wasn't doing enough home schooling. Worried in case my colleagues didn't think I was pulling my weight at home. Worried that I wasn't looking after myself and I'd lose the baby.

The pregnancy continued well. Sadly, my husband couldn't attend any of the scans. Although this was disappointing our main concern was that our baby was alive and growing well. My anxiety throughout the pregnancy was mentally exhausting so we decided to book a private scan at 18 weeks to bridge the gap in NHS scans and to provide some reassurance that everything was ok. It was at this scan I found out we were to have another boy. To be honest, we really didn't mind what we were having as long as it was healthy.

As the months went on I continued working from home until two weeks before my due date. Due to my son's birth by emergency C-section this time I had a planned C-section. My husband was allowed in with me during the birth and we were lucky to have the same doctor who delivered our first child also deliver this one. Restrictions were still in place in hospital so there was no rush of grandparents visiting the day of the birth, instead we face timed to introduce our little man. My husband was allowed to visit between the hours of 2pm-6pm each day.

Once home we settled into our new life as a family of four. It wasn't how we wanted it to be. Family and friends were limited as to when they were allowed round. We had to constantly work out the maths and check we were abiding by the rules. We are lucky that most of our family have met our new addition once. They are desperate to see him grow up, to have those sleepy cuddles, to work out ways to make him chuckle but this is having to be via video call most of the time. We are lucky. We haven't lost anyone close to us to Covid. We all have our health and each other.

In the next month I make my staggered return to work. It's hard not to look back at my maternity leave feeling robbed. We haven't been to a single baby group. We haven't been to Bounce and Rhyme at the local library. We haven't met with friends in coffee shops and eaten cake. We haven't been for the first swim.

Recently I went for another walk. Whilst on this particular walk I noticed lots of new mums also taking their new addition out and it really got me thinking...

I wonder if we would have met at a baby class.
I wonder if we would have chatted in the baby changing areas in our local shopping centre.
I wonder if our little ones would have cooed and smiled at each other during the library story sessions.
I wonder if we would have been mummy friends.

This year has been tough for so many, it has been tough for me, it has been tough for new mums...

So if you see a new mum out on a walk, give them a friendly

smile, you may not know how little sleep she is surviving on and how lonely she is.

No matter how tough the past year has been we will always be grateful for our shining ray of hope, for our rainbow baby, for both of our gorgeous boys.

Tuesday 20th April 2021: Georgina Rouse
1.
Waiting is not a new phenomenon. People often mention the plague or the Spanish flu and what these pandemics taught them about living. However, quite simply, like us, they waited for the worst to pass.

I stayed at home as requested. The whole thing didn't feel real at times. It was removed from me, kept at arm's length. I didn't so much live through it as around it. I never looked it in the eyes.

Sadly, it turned out that the scrolling and tapping and pushing offered no horizon to row towards. We peeked behind the curtain and found there was nothing there that we hadn't seen ourselves. We had thought as much. This time invested was a loss, as some said it would be. We found a current to paddle against but that was about it, although I must say I found the rhythmic motions calming at times.

With nothing to be left out of, we all lived by a familiar tempo. Grocery shop visits and video calls kept us to the same beat, with breaks for an hour or so outside every once in a while. These were kept, though, to known streets and paths. It was numbing, it was wearying. We trod on and it was exhausting.

It turned out that the dread of living without "you'll never guess what" tales was worse than that known fear of missing out. At least we were spared the embarrassment of arriving empty-handed to dinner party silences.

But we faced it, and, in a way, we were together as we hadn't been before. I hope to pack this notion away somewhere safe and keep it to hand. It might come in useful when someone steps on the back of my shoe or races close past on their bike.

2.

My flat is small, and this is now well known to me. Returning from holiday, I sometimes used to open the door and realise my space was much smaller than I had imagined. This feeling now lingers.

Now, I could map the layout with fine detail and retrace my steps around the nooks and crannies. I could give a guided tour of the tiny cracks on walls and the marks in the carpet.

I would never have dreamed of working on the way to the office before. It was something done in movies – something high-flying executives did on the train. But now, it seems, work is let loose and all around us. It's pressing, at times. Others close the door to their spare room office and try not to worry for the evening. Some don't have the real estate. My method is this: in busy periods and the everyday, I build my small walls brick by brick, with whatever I can find lying around.

I have come to create my own liminal spaces wherever possible. I can clean the desk, look at the desk, and be outside of work. I can swipe away an email notification, un-tempted, and be outside of work. I can set out my clothes, hang them up neatly on the wardrobe door and be out of office.

I know now that we set our own boundaries. We all hold the day-job and the position of camp caretaker. Sometimes we must wade through the pressure like thick hail and sometimes we hop through the drizzle over puddles. Sometimes I have even found a ray or two resting on my cheek, warming it gently. I take out the bins in tea breaks and recite my To Do list while I collect the post. In many ways I enjoy being less hurried than before.

Responsibility, too, is everywhere. As are family and belonging. Duty to friends, to loved ones – these things do not stay within their respective spaces or time slots. Besides, it is always there and felt, known, and knowing, lurking in absent-minded pauses and TV binges. "I should message so-and-so" watches over from the corner while we do the washing up. The guilt of an unsent text, or a call shrugged off, slipped by, moved aside – these feelings remain and are cyclical, wherever our relations reside.

We've learned that we set our own boundaries, and we must remember to build windows - gaps for the air to circulate, for the walls to breathe.

3.
At home and nearby I have learned to adapt my presence. I can shrink to the size of a pea in the crowded freezer aisle and bloat when alone to fill an empty room. But, when we go, I will make my body known. I will let myself slip in-between others and swell like a balloon to fill the gaps. I will take the empty seat on the park bench and I will nip into the coffee shop when there's no waiting line. I will hop skip one-two to cross the road and thank the pausing car who lets me by. I will take the whole back row of the bus if I please. I will fill the free space on the grass in the park and I will watch and listen. I will intrude. I will take a double step to fill the cavity in the moving crowd.

I can say now that I am grateful for those who made space for me within their own, sharing their slow Sunday afternoons, hurried catch-ups and fleeting nods, hellos and goodbyes. I am grateful for cafes who let me stay with them for an hour, for a while, in-between moments and on the way elsewhere. I thank those who let me stop to tie my laces, rearrange my handbag, and take a sip of water. I am grateful for shared reactions when car horns sound, or when passers-by drop their phone, trip, or laugh too loudly. I'm thankful for these momentary glances that draw us together. I hope to be kinder when revisiting.

I am most grateful for your hospitality.

Wednesday 21st April 2021: Martin Hales

It's 21st April 2021 - a day to personally reflect on the events of the last 12 months or so.

Doesn't it seem such a long time ago that we all started to become aware of the media stories about a mysterious virus but not really paying that much attention? Couldn't happen here …could it? As days passed into weeks, reality dawned and we were all consumed by talk of a global pandemic and its repercussions.

Back to the beginning. At the start of last year, we were coping with the illness and hospitalisation of my father and the knowledge that we would say an inevitable final goodbye to my father-in-law during the forthcoming months. We had all these thoughts and ideas about how we can help and support them, the things we could all do to create (in one case) some final happy memories.

Simple things were planned but our hopes were shattered by lockdowns, isolation, and distancing.

March 2020 was a time to re-think and reassess. It came down to a simple process. If we maintained our safety, the chances were our parents should also keep safe. But, at the same time we also needed to provide as much comfort and support as we could as we knew coping would be a real challenge for them. And there was still work to think about…

At least there was. Any need to consider work/life balances became irrelevant as furlough started. From that moment there were no other considerations, nothing else mattered other than our families and protecting them. Every day, every week, every month took on a defined form. Some weeks were better than others but all involved unconditional care and support. It was our time to reciprocate and provide.

They needed us now more than ever.

Fortunately, my father's reliance on professional social care was limited and he thankfully improved, notwithstanding the enforced isolation of lockdown that has been a blight on so many including the young and old. For him life changed direction, a 'reset' button was pushed as he and my mother reassessed what they could and now couldn't do. Slowly they adapted to their new normal. They had grown used to independent and active lives. Time had changed, perhaps forever.

As for my father-in-law, as spring turned to summer it became increasingly obvious that what we expected was getting nearer. We were looking at end of life care. His final wishes were to remain at home and it was evident that this would have to be managed primarily by the family. Whilst support was available it was difficult to arrange and at best sporadic, and we were ever anxious to avoid (and indeed dreaded) any enforced separation and isolation from loved ones which was affecting so many.

Sadly, as we moved to autumn, we knew time was not on our side as his life ebbed away. Each added day became a bonus, there were good days that gave us hope which were outweighed by the increasing number of bad days.

The inevitable happened one morning in mid-October.

Much of that period remains a blur but some things remain very clear. I sit here today reflecting, trying to think of the right words.

Whilst we both made a commitment to do whatever we had to do to look after our families what happened in the last few difficult days with very limited professional support defied description. It was extraordinary. I saw up close what I shall always know: my wife is truly amazing with virtually unlimited resources of selfless, unconditional love. The total support she and other family members provided to her father over the last weeks of his life and subsequently, continuously to her surviving mother has been nothing short of phenomenal. We talk much about heroes and heroines. Many of them are closer than we think.

She helped give her father a precious gift denied to so many in 2020 – a peaceful, serene death in the company of loved ones. Family where life begins and love never ends.

It's very easy to dwell on the negatives but I suspect what we went through created many positives and taught us valuable lessons in life and despite everything the last year wasn't without elements of fun and laughter. Perhaps less so than other years but it still had its 'lighter' moments.

On reflection it certainly gave me time to consider what is actually important, it certainly made me re-assess my priorities. It changed me. I'm sure those changes will create the building blocks for our future. I suspect I am not the only person who at the onset and during successive lockdowns felt slightly overwhelmed by what was ahead of us, what we had to do and anxious as to what the future may bring. Despite adversity we talked, we coped, we supported, and sometimes (without saying a word) just put our arms around each other: we were there for each other.

Perhaps now there is light at the end of this long tunnel and we can all start to move forward. What the new normal will be is anyone's guess but the one thing I take away from this year is that I now understand that as I grow older it isn't about the material things… it's about what's in our hearts and who we care for. We have to cherish every single moment where we are able to be with the ones we love. It's over all too quickly.

In the words of C S Lewis 'You can't go back and change the beginning but you can start where you are and change the ending'.

Thursday 22nd April 2021: Neil Staveley

At the end of 2018 I wasn't in a good place with my mental health. I knew if I didn't make some changes, things would go downhill very quickly. So, I decided to quit my job of 24 years, and run from Switzerland back to Dereham in Norfolk. But that's a different story.

How is this relevant to 2020? At the same time as quitting my job, I decided to do something incredibly scary – start my own business, doing something I was passionate about. The one thing that always helped with my mental health was running, so I started up a trail running business. The whole ethos of the business would be to organise running events that would help people escape the stresses of everyday life.

After much planning, I was finally ready to hold my first event, which would take place on the 14th March 2020. As the event got closer, I experienced a mixture of nerves and utter excitement; this was what I'd dreamed of, what I'd gambled pretty much everything on – job security, financial security, and, of course, my mental health.

I was aware of a virus in China, but that was miles away, right? We didn't need to worry, did we? Then, before my big first event, cases were confirmed in the UK. All of a sudden I wasn't even sure if I would be able to hold the event. I spent hours checking the news, checking guidelines, hoping that I wouldn't be affected. Being outside and able to distance ourselves from each other, I knew the risks at my event were low, but I suddenly had the worry – what if someone became ill after attending my event, or worse, how would I cope with that? Luckily, although we had to socially distance, the event could go ahead (looking back, was this the right thing to do, who knows?) It was a fantastic success, and I was feeling the proudest and happiest I think I ever have.

Then, two days later, a national lockdown was announced. Just like that, those feelings of excitement, and confidence that I could make a go of this new business, disappeared. Would I and my family stay safe? Would my new business survive? Would I lose everything financially?

The worry of suddenly having no income, worrying about my family and friends, the guilt of worrying about money when people were facing much worse, inevitably sent my mental health on a sharp downward spiral. Ironically, the name of my new business was ESCAPE trails, and this was the one thing I now couldn't do. But I started receiving messages of support from family, friends, customers, and from the fantastic members of my running club, the Norfolk Gazelles. Slowly I started to get the determination back that I could make a go of this; having no idea at the time that this support would keep me going for the next year!

The year 2020 became a cycle of lockdowns lifting, checking guidance from the Government and the sports' governing body, organising small events, getting excited, lockdowns coming into place, cancelling events, emailing customers to apologise for cancelling events, giving refunds, lockdown lifting, checking guidance, organising events, being able to hold events (yay!), seeing customers having great fun at something I'd organised, lots of smiles, then lockdowns coming into place..........an endless cycle of happiness, hope, and complete despair.

It's now April 22nd 2021, and I am surviving, my business is still surviving. I have a small Covid secure event happening in a couple of days' time, and I can't wait. I can finally start helping people escape the stresses of what has very quickly become normal life. I'm looking forward to seeing huge smiley, socially distanced faces. Currently my mental health is very good, but when I look in the mirror I see a lot more lines on my face, and a loooooot more grey hairs.

Knowing now how 2020 was going to turn out, do I regret throwing everything I had at keeping a new business going during a global pandemic? Not at all. In all honesty, I believe if I hadn't, my mental health would have been in a much worse place. And, well, the worst could have happened. Those smiley faces, and the support I've received, quite often from people going through their own struggles, has made me more determined than ever to keep helping people 'escape'.

Friday 23 April 2021: Sharon Clifton

As I sit here reflecting on the past 12 months, it's hard to process just exactly what has happened, not only nationally and internationally with the pandemic, but also personally. Nothing will ever go back to exactly how it was, and everyone is coming to terms with a new reality.

A week after I wrote my reflections last year, saying how lonely I was, I met someone online who I'd met three years earlier, almost to the day, in a recording studio.

We got chatting online and it felt so easy. He was the company I had been craving. We had lots of telephone calls, online drinks dates and when we could, went out for socially distanced walks. It was a strange start to a relationship. When we came out of the first lockdown, we met up and have barely been apart since. By the time of the second lockdown, we had taken the decision to live with each other, as we couldn't bear to be apart, and he was already in a bubble with his mum. It certainly speeded up our courtship.

Little did I know that having him by my side, along with my faithful little dog Jasper, would be how I would get through the next few months.

I was visiting my parents twice weekly to check on them and get any shopping they needed. Mum's Alzheimer's was getting worse and she was suffering with more seizures, despite being on medication for them. The strain was starting to show on my dad. After a particularly bad episode I called for an ambulance. Mum went into hospital. We couldn't go with her. She had long lost the ability to express herself meaningfully and I was scared they wouldn't understand her needs. But they got her seizures under control. The big shock came when they said that she wouldn't be able to come home. They felt that she needed respite care as Dad was doing his best, but her needs were beyond what any single person could provide. She went into care at the end of May. We couldn't see her – only through a window and she was unable to communicate or recognise us without physical touch, so it was just too distressing. Dad felt that she had been taken from him. I understood how he felt, but also knew that she needed the extra one-to-one care that she could have in the home. She was safe.

Dad didn't cope well. In their 60 years of marriage they had never been apart. It was heart-breaking to watch. She was his world and for the past six years or so he had done everything for her.

His health deteriorated rapidly. He tried to keep himself occupied, but he was lonely, was becoming increasingly confused and angry, and saw no point in doing anything. He just wanted his wife back.

The summer came, we ate out to help out. We walked lots. We worked hard – mostly at home, which I found a lonely experience that didn't help my own mental health. Endless Zoom and Teams calls featuring various pets and every meeting you would hear the phrase 'you're on mute'. We were all making the best of a strange and challenging situation which we never believed would go on as long as it has.

In September, Reg, Jasper and I went to the peak district. It was a beautiful week. It felt almost normal. We had meals out, mooched around shops that were open, and walked miles. Dad was ringing me several times a day. He was getting himself so muddled. I was worried that he was starting to show signs of dementia. The stress of it was starting to take its toll on me, but I did what I could to listen and be patient.

When I got home I visited Dad and it was clear that he was actually very poorly. I couldn't get a GP to see him in person.

We tried to do a video consultation, but he was deaf so that was very difficult, and the GP wasn't able to hear how poor Dad's breathing was. In the end I called an ambulance again. I had a very bad feeling about it, after what had happened with Mum, and was terrified that I wouldn't see my dad again.

It turned out that Dad had pneumonia. Somehow, with treatment, he managed to get over it. The hospital wanted to discharge him home, but I said "he isn't able to care for himself, he is very confused". He was using a stick then and barely able to walk. I insisted that he was seen by the lung consultant he had seen previously. I met the consultant after he saw my dad and was informed that dad had terminal lung cancer and only about six weeks to live. The news floored me. I knew he had an issue with his lung, but I wasn't prepared for that news. He was also showing signs of vascular dementia. End of life care in a local care home was arranged. Thankfully my sister and I could visit him every day. We were at his beside holding his hands when he passed five weeks later. Just before he passed, I was able to tell him that a great grandchild was on the way, that I was to be a grandma for the first time. It was real circle of life stuff.

Then came the funeral with limited numbers and no wake. It felt like we hadn't really said goodbye properly, even though the service was exactly what he would have wanted – fuss free.

The next dilemma – do we tell Mum? How do you explain to someone that they have lost someone they don't even remember? We decided not to. Why cause any unnecessary stress. She was happy in her world, oblivious to it all.

Personally, the biggest thing for me over the last year is the moments that we've lost that we can't get back. I feel like I have lost my mum and didn't really get to say goodbye. My dad never got to say goodbye. How could he have known that when she got in the ambulance it would be the last time he saw her? I have missed birthdays with my family. I have missed watching my grandchild grow in mummy's tummy. I have missed watching the excitement on my son's face.

What I have learned is to value every precious moment, and to say the things you need to say, don't wait for the right moment – it may never come. I have not kept in touch with friends because I felt I had nothing positive to say. Now I realise I should have made more of an effort. We could have helped each other through the more challenging days. Friends, family, and my partner are more important than anything else. This pandemic has really brought that home to me.

I am eternally grateful to Reg who has seen me through all of this.

Saturday 24th April 2021: Tony Hall

It has been the strangest of times, many people across the world have sadly lost their lives, lost their loved ones through this pandemic. I hold this thought as I write about my time during lockdown.

I had been planning to retire and made my decision known to my organisation just after Christmas 2020, agreeing to work until July 2021. Like most people I could not believe the events that unfolded during last spring as we organised working from home and board meetings via Zoom. The team were fantastic and I am proud of the service we were able to continue providing for our tenants.

In parallel to this, I had to get my head around retiring. Firstly, although I loved my job, I wanted the time and space to do the things that I had not had the chance to do for years. Despite everything, the team gave me a great send off, lots of kind messages. I turned sixty, no party on this occasion, but we found ways of connecting with friends and family. People made every effort to do want they could to get in touch which has been one of the positive points coming out of this time. If you cannot do what you planned, what can you do?

When systems and processes are under pressure cracks appear. It exposes weaknesses and risks and we question why things are like they are; how care is provided for old and vulnerable people, how our food is produced and processed, how we use and abuse the environment. During my working life regulation was frustrating at time. Last night I watched a film, 'Dark Waters'. It was about how DuPont behaved right up until 2015 and regulation failed everyone. It's worth watching. My hope is that when we emerge from this terrible virus, we can get the balance right between social and business needs.

Going back to plans, it was always my plan to have a boat in my retirement, I love being on the water. I had always thought it would be sea-going, my wife didn't, so, we compromised. I now have a beautiful river boat, which I am now sat on sharing these thoughts. It will slow me down and help me stop to take in more of the world around me. I am really looking forward to the summer on the river and a simpler way of life.

Sunday 25th April 2021: Sarah Dennis

Well, here we are again – one year on from the last time I shared my reflections in the first When The World Paused diary. Who would have thought we would still be in the midst of a pandemic after all this time? The last time I wrote I genuinely thought it would all be over by June 2020. Soon we'd be back to seeing friends and family. Booking a holiday. Giving everyone a hug. But it was not to be.

Life has changed so much. I work in a busy office, normally full of hundreds of people, but the last year has seen the office devoid of staff, most of us working from home at least a couple of days a week. It's become like the Marie Celeste. King's Lynn town centre was like something from an apocalyptic film. On one day there was just me, in the whole of the high street. Very strange indeed.

Life certainly became less busy – no visits to or from friends or family, no days or meals out. And of course, worse than any of that, the daily death toll. Always one to avoid watching the news, it was hard to miss the pain and suffering of families losing loved ones in such an unexpected way. Friends told me stories of people admitted to hospital with a broken ankle and never coming home again, having caught Covid.

Each week seemed to provide a new set of rules and restrictions. Due to a lack of the news in my house, I took to asking one of my colleagues every Monday "What can't I do this week?!" I just didn't want to face the reality; it was far too scary. My partner was working away which made life that bit harder, but he was in a country with very little Covid, so at least he was safe. But the problem with seeing fewer and fewer people and doing less and less is that it eventually turns you into a bit of a hermit! Working at home isn't my cup of tea, especially when you're on your own, and you find yourself talking to the resident spiders.

I lost two relatives last year, neither from Covid, but mourning the loss of loved ones was difficult due to restrictions in place. I felt for new mums, giving birth without their partners beside them. A very sociable friend of mine had her second child in lockdown and spent many frustrating and isolating months looking after a toddler and a newborn. I could only imagine how hard that was. People's mental health has suffered, along with the physical suffering, and the legacy of this will continue for some time, I'm sure. I wonder how young children will remember this time? A friend of mine was telling me that her little niece panics slightly when anyone gets too close and how confusing the whole 'bubble' thing must be. I find myself gasping out loud at the TV when people get too close to each other – "No! You can't do that!" Until you realise that this was a time when you could.

But every so often there was light at the end of the tunnel. Shops started to re-open, we could socialise (just a bit) and of course the summer came along and sunny days make everyone feel better don't they? We were given a day with family and friends at Christmas which was fabulous! And now the shops are re-opening and everyone seems so much more cheerful. And a haircut and colour! Ok, I know that's vain but oh, what a difference that made! A bit of normality in a very odd year. The world will have changed so much due to Covid, in more ways than I will ever be aware of. Some of this I'm hoping for the better.

I read somewhere that the sales of false eyelashes has rocketed and sales of lipstick have plummeted. Well, I am doing my best for lipstick sales and refuse to stop wearing it, just because I'm wearing a mask. I think we are more resilient than we realise – just think of the last year, and we've nearly made it through. I'm keeping everything crossed that my partner will finish his work overseas and flights will get back to normal so he can get home when he plans to, and not days of delays and umpteen Covid tests. Let's hope that June really does see an end to all restrictions and we can all go back to our normal.

Monday 26th April 2021: Ange Fox

PING… one of my new favourite sounds, my heart jumps… a simple little 'PING' and yet behind that little 'PING' will often be a one-line text message on my phone: 'Fancy a walk…?' Oooooh, do I! My daughter Abbie is heading out with Walter, her ten-month-old adorable cocker spaniel. I soon bounce into action, it's all systems go, pulling on shoes and grabbing my jacket and a few dog treats, quick wee, and then I'm out of the door like a bat out of hell! Whatever I am doing, a walk with those two little delights is just like the best thing ever right now. Ian, the hubster, has become accustomed to me suddenly flying out of the front door at the drop of a hat, meals have been put on hold, baths turned cold, conversations dropped as soon as that little 'PING' pings in – I'm outta there. These mum and daughter walks are so very precious, we put the world to rights on these little walks, we listen to each other's worries and strifes and our hearts burst at the joyous things we sometimes share.

Abbie and my son-in-law Scott moved to within an eight-minute walk door to door from our house to theirs at the end of November last year, and oh my goodness, it's heaven on earth – or it would be if I could get inside for a proper mooch around. The very first thing I'll be doing when restrictions are lifted is getting inside. I've had video tours of course but hugs and squeezes aside I just want to sit on their sofa with them, rummage through their cupboards (I jest… or do I?!!) quite normal little things but honestly it will be just so, so lovely to have the freedom to do them. It's such a massive thing to move house and to move during lockdown even more so, hats off to them and to anyone moving house during lockdown. A week after their move, Abbie had a positive Covid test, this was a shocker to us all, most of all to Abbie as she is the most 'on-it' person I know. It was so tough for them and heart wrenching all around as the very little contact that we had been managing to have during this Covid stricken world was suddenly whipped away. Thank heavens for technology is all I can say but even then when you're feeling as rough as anything you hardly want to be chatting away to your mother on FaceTime. Ho Hum!! They were troopers and got through this hurdle and what we gained from this experience is to not take anything for granted and hence every chance of a little walk we grab them, precious moments.

Let's talk about the Fitbit challenge. PING… this time a message on my Fitbit app… 'Liam W has invited you to join the Workweek Hustle'. My heart jumps again even though he invites me practically every week, I still get that rush of excitement every time that message pops in. I have occasionally snuck in and beat him to it by inviting him first but more often than not he's ahead of me on that one. I don't very often stand a chance of winning this challenge as my son Liam works in football. He's Head of Performance Analysis for Al Wahda, a team over in Abu Dhabi. He does lots of training with the team, he has two gorgeous little stepsons and spends lots of time chasing around with them, he naturally gets a lot of steps in during the challenge. One of the rare times that I have managed to beat him was when he was having to isolate in a hotel due to a few of the team members having positive Covid results, he had to stay in his room. HA!! Go me!! The Fitbit challenge is a wonderful way for Liam and I to have a connection while he's so far away, we have a lot of banter along the way too, it's fun. We haven't physically seen each other since Abbie and Scott's wedding way back in August 2019. I have a little consistent ache in my heart from missing him, his smashing wife Claire, and the boys but I am thankful that they are safe and happy and we are getting nearer to a time when we can safely and comfortably travel once more, fingers crossed. I visualise the hugs we'll be having when we finally get together again, I cry now every time we speak. Well, not while we're speaking but as soon as the phone call ends I burst into tears, no controlling my emotions, Ian is at the ready with a massive hug, funny how he always just 'knows'. Technology once again has been my saviour, mostly the Fitbit but also WhatsApp chattering and of course heart lifting Zoom calls.

When I wrote for the first When The World Paused diary exactly a year ago to the day it was an excruciatingly sad, sad time as we'd just lost Ian's wonderful dad to cancer. It's been hard. Furlough for me was like a gift, the gift of time, I was able to be there for Ian's mum and it was so comforting to do so and not worry about work. I'm forever grateful that I was given that time, I have no idea how we would have survived without it. Ian's mum has been so incredibly brave, if I told you everything about this remarkable woman I would be here writing for a month of Sundays but I will just say she's a true trojan.

Bubbles! We have both our mums in our bubble, how lucky are we! Easing out of furlough and back into work at first hit very hard, I absolutely love my job but juggling work with looking out for both mums was no mean feat. My mum thinks I've been helping her get through these wretched days but actually she's been helping me too, she's such great company, her sense of humour is like no other, she very quick witted, fun, and just lovely to be around. I am now in a bit of a routine and everything is working out swimmingly. Now that people can meet up outdoors we have garden visits happening so the mums are having more company, a saving grace really as I fear I'm beginning to get on their chimes. My mum has actually said to me more than once "I think I'd like to change my bubble" and I'd reply "That'll be great Mum," and we've both laughed, she's hilarious!

PING... sorry, gotta go...

Tuesday 27th April 2021: Serena Grant
Wow – so 2020, what a year!

I always thought 2020 was going to be an amazing year – it just has that ring to it doesn't it.

Unfortunately in January 2020, my grandad passed away. Work wise though, everything was looking hopeful – I had filled the calendar for pretty much every single weekend and had numerous weddings booked over the summer, as well as festivals across the country. Everything was looking really positive and I was so excited about the new opportunities.

Suddenly Covid happened. It hit me really hard. I went from being full of hope to losing everything – 250+ gigs cancelled, all my income lost (as being a musician is my only job), my mortgage lender pulled out of the sale on a flat I'd been approved to buy and I lost that, as well as the already paid solicitor fees etc. I became really down and struggled, and it really affected my mental state.

Then, I gave myself something to focus on and it really helped. I suddenly got the motivation to write a charity song – I got other musicians involved, all recording from home, and had 50+ people (and animals!) included in the music video which I created also. Then, there was the publicising of it and getting it out there which really put my mind to something positive. It lifted my spirits and it felt good helping others too. I learnt that if you put your mind to something, whatever it is, you can make it happen.

I needed something to focus on and put my mind to when I was feeling particularly down. I played about on my keyboard and came up with some basic chords, and then thought through the lyrics. Whilst lying in bed that night, I thought, wouldn't it be lovely to make this into a charity single and raise money for the NHS who have done and are doing such an amazing job. And the next day I started the project properly and got to work. It certainly exceeded my expectations in a sense that so many people wanted to be involved and it made me feel really honoured that they wanted to be involved in my idea!

Musicians flocked to Facebook Live when lockdown was announced. I used to do a live stream every week from the sofa. I really enjoyed it, and people were kind and generous. But after a while, life went back to normal for a lot of people and my views went down. When pubs reopened, I was super excited to get back out there and start gigging again. I was over the moon and contacted many venues, and I did get quite a few gigs booked in, especially in some lovely pub gardens and even socially distanced festivals. Some weddings even still went ahead – I performed on a boat on the Norfolk Broads on a seven-hour cruise for a small wedding celebration! Then there was the 10pm curfew, and the cold weather outside, bookings dropped significantly, and the winter and Christmas - which last year was my busiest and most profitable time - became quite bleak.

My nan also became ill during this time and sadly passed away. Losing two family members, all of my income, my mortgage (and relationship issues which I won't go into) hit me incredibly hard and I became incredibly low. Seeking help from friends, and also writing another song, is what ultimately helped me through during this difficult time.

2021 happened. I was glad to see the back of 2020! But everyone seemed so positive about 2021 – even though things have pretty much been the same! However, this year I have felt much more positive and have put 2020 behind me! In January, out of the blue I had an enquiry from an agency about doing a 'doorstep gig'. I'd never heard of these before, and spoke to the client to find out more. She was from London, and apparently doorstep gigs had become very popular in the city. I went ahead with the gig, and was surprised how well it went. She encouraged me to advertise – she also recommended me herself following on from her performance. I was lucky enough to then have a flood of enquiries for socially distanced doorstep gigs – and I was over the moon to have been able to adapt my work into something where I could still gig, which boosted my confidence, and deliver a 'gift' to a loved one from someone who wasn't able to travel because of the lockdown. I felt so blessed to bring joy to people's special day. I was so grateful to have that opportunity – selfishly, it boosted my morale.

Additionally, I also offered online Zoom parties – setting up a gig from home and live streaming it – it was so lovely to find alternative ways to perform and bring live music to people's living rooms. I really enjoyed these times and I'm so pleased I was able to turn 2021 into a more positive year than previously.

I built up my little business from nothing and, especially over the last couple of years, have been really pleased with how well things have been going and so proud of how far things have gone and given me the opportunities that I've worked so hard for. I even had an employee working for me too – and was approved for a mortgage as a self-employed individual which I never thought would be possible! I just hope that things will get better soon for all musicians, and the whole entertainment industry for that matter – as what is life without music?

Luckily I have been able to perform in pubs and bars (albeit outside!) the last couple of weeks and hopefully things will pick up – I have most of my diary for the summer full! Let's just keep staying safe and fingers crossed the cases will go down and we can all go back to the 'new normal'.

Wednesday 28th April 2021: Lucy Wigley

In the weeks prior to the first lockdown, I very much played Queen Ostrich in full denial by totally burying my head in the sand. Every week that the schools threatened to close and didn't gave my neck muscles an increase in brute strength to keep forcing my head into that sand. I tried to make myself believe this pandemic was somehow going to apologise for its unwanted presence and potential disruption to my life and retreat back under its rock. The thing is, I'm not very good with change; really not good at all. I'd like to swagger forth and confidently announce that I'm dynamic and adaptable and nothing fazes me, like I'm vomiting out words from the world's most predictable CV. The truth is that I'd rather eat the same foods every day at the same times, and not have my routine disrupted.

The two things that really stick in my head from that time are that I became strangely obsessed with snacks, and watching social distancing in a busy urban area of the city – where I happen to live – was the closest thing I had to a real-life comedy sketch. People ninja rolling into bushes to get out of the way of others, and doing what I came to call the 'panic jig' around each other to try and decide how to best move around each other while keeping the distance. It reminded me of Super Mario, where you have to jump out of the way of those pesky mushrooms in case they should – gasp – touch you and finish you off. Perhaps I should mention that since childhood I've also turned pretty much every situation into comedy, no matter how serious, which is an actual valid coping mechanism.

We entered home school with gusto and with the weather practically Mediterranean, we sort of managed. Alas, home schooling soon wore thin and before long, nobody really cared or had the energy to care about how many apples Billy had if he started with 11, his dog ate one, he was so bored he threw six into his neighbour's garden and his frazzled mum used two as stress balls. I can't remember who gave up first, us or them, it was a kind of chicken/egg situation. I began frantically googling 'when will Coronavirus end' and other very similar sentences using a mixture of different words, like I was putting key phrases through a research database for a thesis. I think I actually hoped that I'd get an answer similar to: 'next Wednesday it will all be over'. No matter how many times I told myself that I was lucky – I had a safe home, my husband at home to help me, and that there were people much worse off than myself and I needed to think of them and stop being selfish, I couldn't help the part of myself that just needed normality.

The second lockdown, although I was more prepared and had been expecting it, was just as hard. I'm a self-employed freelancer, and my work had dried up completely during lockdown one as the businesses I worked for prioritised their employed staff, and freelancers were the first to go. I had worked really hard to get my work back up and running, and did not want to let it all go again. My children were also gutted about being away from their friends and their routines for the second time, refusing home school flat out, and began openly displaying their anger; I winced as their behaviour and personalities changed in front of me. The more sunshine and rainbows part of these reflections is coming, don't worry, but despite trying to be fun mum who tried everything to make the time even a little joyous, the predominant memories are that it was bleak and miserable.

Now for the teachable moment! Last week we went on our first holiday since last summer, and here's what changed: I appreciated it, every moment. Long days were spent at the beach where the children went crabbing, and they got through every single spare bit of clothing I took with us by throwing themselves repeatedly in the sea or rolling in something filthy.

Normally I would have worried about how I was going to get everything clean and dry, but I brushed it off. My need to cling to routine sees me find it nearly impossible to let the children alter their bedtime, but we all stayed up late, playing games and finding TV shows we could all watch together, instead of me hoping they'd sleep so that I could watch something with zombies or swearing. Sitting outside a restaurant and freezing, but being next to a beautiful river, and eating fresh fish and appreciating every bite, nearly felt like being given a new chance at life – I know, this is getting into dangerous schmaltzy territory, but it's true.

Seeing my children's faces as they run out of school with their friends, and put down the iPads they became dependent on, to make way for pillow fights and trips to the park, fills me with equal relief and joy. They need their friends and their routine just as much as I do. They need time away from me as much as I need head space too, and we can all come together and appreciate time spent together that isn't time spent forced together. I'm not one for making sweeping assertions about making permanent life changes; previous experience has shown me that I'm not good at it, and I only feel I've let myself down when I can't stick to the changes I've promised myself I'll make. I have learned that I need a lot of my own space, but that doesn't make me love and need my family any less. I only hope that the smells and tastes of freedom will stay with me for our next holiday and beyond, and that one day my pride will let me let go of failing at KS2 English AND Maths…

Thursday 29th April 2021: Emma Cluett

Like many others I entered the new decade excited about the year ahead. 2020 was the year I turned 40, and rather than sulk into my wine about the event, I had decided that we would celebrate with many trips abroad and swanky meals out. I had just landed a secondment role in Germany with work and I was looking forward to seeing a lot of the country and trying to convince the team there that, although I should be finished by May, really they needed me out for Oktoberfest to support in some way…

Steins of beer and navigating Ryanair's luggage policy turned out to be the least of my concerns.

I sit here today, recovering from major surgery (knowing that this will be easier to recover from than home-schooling my son!). Strange to say I feel as positive and hopeful about the future as I did when I was popping that champagne cork on New Year's Eve 2019.

2020 turned out not to be the year of trips to Monte Carlo and Australia, but instead a year where I got excited about going to a garden centre and finally, after only 40 years learned to bake.

When lockdown came in March I was optimistic that we would still be having our holidays and meals out in the autumn. Zoom calls were almost exciting and my friends and I enjoyed using novelty backgrounds to pretend that we were on a yacht in Monte Carlo. The weather obliged, by also pretending that it was in Monte Carlo, my husband and I embarked on all the garden DIY projects that we had been "meaning to get on with" for the past 12 years…

My 40th birthday came and was marked by the government as the 'peak of wave 1'. I had a wonderful day, despite the highlight being our 'one walk'. I had no expectations and my friends and family blew me away with all the thoughtful arrangements they had made.

The summer came and everything began to slowly open. My Germany secondment had been extended and I was finally able to get over to the country again. Like many other people I considered the worst was behind us. What a weird few months hey, thank goodness I never have to do home-schooling again…

And then the autumn hit. As well as a second coronavirus wave I was also dealing with a personal 'second wave' and news of a new variant. My uncle had died the year before of cancer which had led to some genetic testing. It identified that our family carried a defect in one of the cancer genes. To my horror, next steps found that my mother also had this, as well as my younger sister. The shock of two of the people I was closest to in the world being identified as having an up to 85% chance of breast cancer hit me harder than finding out the inevitable: I also had the gene defect. Luckily, modern science is amazing, and I couldn't believe how swiftly the three of us were navigated through the health service, seeing various counsellors, and undergoing numerous bouts of screening.

Mum had her ovaries removed due to the heightened risk of ovarian cancer. She coped with this like the stoic superhero I knew she would be despite not being able to have any visitors at the hospital due to the lockdown restrictions. My sister and I underwent breast screening. We both had every test the NHS could throw at us. We joked that having the BRCA gene was the world's crappiest VIP pass for treatment. What was first an inconvenience turned into a scary reality when the screening showed that I had early-stage breast cancer. Everything happened in a blur and in March this year I had a double mastectomy with immediate reconstruction.

Today is six weeks since my operation and marks the day I can finally drive and run again! It is remarkable the same things that you take for granted and the freedoms that you have that you don't even realise. As I hit the milestones on my recovery, I was grateful. Grateful to be able to shower myself, pull myself out of my chair, hold my dog to take him for a walk, hug my children without worry it would hurt me.

It strikes me how lucky I am and have been. Lucky to have an uncle who in his last days pushed for genetic testing, knowing that something wasn't right, and determined to ensure his family had the best possible chance. Without the knowledge that this genetic testing found I would never have been screened and caught the cancer. Lucky to have our NHS. Everyone says it, I'm not sure I really understood how good our health service is until the last few months and how talented and caring they all are.

 Above all else I am incredibly lucky to have the family and friends that I do. The unwavering support, albeit mostly from a social distance was overwhelming. The runs and dog walks with my best friends where I cried it out, my mum, dad and sister rallying around and keeping so strong, and of course my children and husband. I am the world's worst patient, yet my husband kept calm and strong, looking after me as well as keeping life normal for the children. I hope if I ever need to repay the favour I do as well as he did, I have my doubts…

I was told two weeks ago that the cancer hadn't spread, and I needed no further treatment. Cheers to the last year, I can't pretend it's been anyone's best year, but it's certainly taught me a lot, (and that's just the home-schooling part!)

Friday 30th April 2021: Hannah Freeman
Wow. Where to start.

These past 12 months have been filled with so much, yet so much has been taken away.

When I spotted a request for guest writers for this journal, I jumped at the chance. Why? Because throughout the pandemic I haven't jotted down any thoughts, feelings, or memories from this period in our lifetime. Choosing to ignore the enormity of it perhaps. But to pause, write and reflect on this time is important. For others to learn from, but also to make sense of it for ourselves.

Yes, I've Instagrammed (mainly the good bits, don't we all!), made the odd Facebook post, and close friends and family have umpteen voice tags and WhatsApp messages from me, sharing the highs and lows of daily lockdown life. On good days: "We've been for a midday walk at the beach and it was beautiful, lockdown life isn't so bad after all." And on the not so good: "Send help, send wine – bl***y Beowulf is on the timetable again today!" But that's how I've sporadically documented this experience. I'm not one for keeping a diary or journaling. So here goes. An honest reflection, recollection, and very likely rambling account of a year in lockdown.

Flashback to March 2020, and a stand-out memory is having a little cry at my youngest daughter's gymnastics club. Yes, the tears started then. And have been a regular occurrence ever since. Anyone who knows me well knows I'm not a crier. But boy, this lockdown got me. It's been emotional!

22 March 2020, the day before THAT announcement. We knew it was coming. But equally, I could not quite comprehend it. My youngest daughter (five at the time) was enjoying, what I knew would be, her last gymnastics class for a while. The thing she loves most to do. The coaches knew it

too. I watched on from the balcony as the children teared around the hall playing hide and seek, the giggles spilling out and echoing in the eerily quiet gymnasium, ordinarily packed with chattering parents. I sat there solo and shed a tear. Kids being kids - when would they get the chance again? Our school had already decided to close, and now the children's clubs would too. It didn't seem right; their fun, their friends, were all being snatched away. But, of course, it needed to happen. National lockdown was imminent. A fortnightly supermarket trip soon to be my only form of real-life social interaction.

The following day it dawned on my eldest daughter (eight years old) that her dance lessons too would be no more, or at least for the time being. Cue watery eyes again from her and from me.

Those two moments really stick in my memory. When the penny dropped, my young children couldn't quite understand why this was happening. I couldn't really explain without risk of frightening them. And my heart sank.

As we processed the unfathomable school closures, daily life being put under the control of government restrictions, children, and us both at home 24/7, next came work. I love my job. I love what we do. But with major client PR projects and events postponed, stalled, or cancelled and clients, as we all were, uncertain about what the future held, I was furloughed. Not working is alien to me (I've always had a job since I was 16). So, I threw myself into my new 'role' of year 1 and year 3 teacher. Before quickly realising that spending every Sunday night planning timetables and arranging teaching resources on the kitchen table would be better spent in a hot bath, plastered in a face mask, and with wine in hand.

Despite what can only be described as a 'winging it' approach to home-schooling, the girls coped incredibly well, and come lockdown two (the sequel) we'd all learnt that I was willing and able to teach English and History, Dad's skills were in Maths and Science, and once enthusiasm waned, we could always fall back on arts, crafts (tie-dye t-shirts, air-dry clay – in my element!), playing outside (the trampoline – wisest buy ever), reading (a renewed love for me), and baking. Of which, we did A LOT! (I say 'we', my eldest took the lead, I supervised, while my youngest was chief spoon licker).

But while all this was going on, in the background we faced another unsettling twist in the rollercoaster of coronavirus life.

After Christmas, we'd learnt my dad was quite seriously unwell. So unwell in fact he needed surgery to remove a kidney. It was urgent, but Covid doesn't consider that. And all pre-op appointments were cancelled. It was incredibly worrying but we and he were incredibly lucky. A private hospital, thankfully, started acting as a satellite site for NHS patients who needed urgent treatment, and within days of a call, he was taken in for his first op there. A few weeks later, and he was booked in at the Norfolk & Norwich University Hospital for his kidney to be removed, just as the second wave of the pandemic started to dip. We know how fortunate he was. To be operated on. And to escape Covid, returning home to recover in full. Seeing the waiting list figures now is scary. We count our lucky stars.

It was an awful, worrying time. Two periods in hospital. No visitors allowed. My mum dropping him at the door, to be taken into the caring, wonderful hands of our NHS. Talking to him only on FaceTime. It wasn't an experience he or we would wish to repeat. Or see anyone else encounter alone. But we really are grateful that his operation went ahead, despite the massive strain and pressures on the NHS at this time, and he has recovered. We know so many others who have not had this run of good fortune, and who continue to wait; sick with worry.

Going through that, in the middle of an unpredictable, worrying time, made us appreciate each other and the simple things all the more.

And as soon as lockdown one was lifted, and UK holidays were back on the cards, we booked a much-needed family staycation in Wales. Where we met up with my Cardiff-residing sister for the first time in months.

A cottage in Wales, in the middle of lush green hills, with nothing much to fill our time other than visiting castle ruins, eating long lazy breakfasts together, making dens in the girls' bedroom, playing dominoes, and browsing market stalls was just what the doctor ordered. The trip finished with my girls, my sister, and brother-in-law wild swimming in the river as I watched on from the bank, their faces lit with beaming grins (or were they grimaces from the cold? Hard to tell from my sunbathing spot!). We were meant to be in Kos. I wouldn't have swapped it.

And while away on that holiday, another chapter in our lockdown story began. Browsing online, we found a breeder local to us with Cavapoo puppies. We booked a visit and met our puppy in July. Instant love. Buddy arrived home in September. Yes, we're a Covid cliché, but he was always meant to be a part of our family.

Throughout the summer, we made the most of every moment outdoors. With sandy beaches, marshes thriving with nature and woodland walks on our doorstep, I repeated daily "we're so lucky to live where we do." And we really are. I've appreciated our spot in Suffolk so much more. And will continue to do so, long after this time has passed.

And I think that is my big lockdown life lesson. To never to take this lovely life and the people we love for granted. To slow life down, take in the moments that matter and don't overcomplicate it. Do what makes you and the people you love the hardest happy.

Perhaps it is because I am creeping towards a big birthday, my girls are seemingly transforming into mini teens before my eyes and I wish time could take on a gentler pace more permanently, but I now know that a slower, less complicated life is good. And that will stick with me. The pandemic has taken so much away, but by stripping things right back, it's also given us the chance to pause, reflect and revaluate. What a gift.

404 days have passed since I blubbed as I watched on in the gymnastics hall. Yesterday, I dropped my youngest daughter off there for her tumbling lessons. They've been back a couple of weeks. And my eldest has returned to the dance studio, awaiting results from a tap exam taken last week, a year later than originally planned.

Life is gradually returning to normal. The girls are happy to be back with friends and doing the things they love. As am I. But as we move ahead, I'm very happy and ready to approach it from the slow and steady lane.

Saturday 1st May 2021: Lara Laing

Not many people know this but me and Boris Johnson are going to get married. This is the world according to my 5-year-old daughter Bobbi. Every time I receive a letter or Boris is on the TV, Bobbi raises her eyebrows and says: "Look Mum, it's Boris". Apparently we are both going to live at number 10 and Daddy can come too.

These little moments are what has kept me and hubby going through the last year, kids are hard work but they are blooming funny too!

I look back on this time last year and lockdown was still a novelty and we were enjoying living off BBQs, and making the most of our daily exercise, having virtual drinks and Zoom quizzes.

Now I'm bored of it all, I think we all are, winter lockdown was tough and quite often I would just burst into tears and say to my husband Dave: "I'm sick of the living room and every day merging into one."

So I decided we needed to get out of this funk that we have found ourselves in, on a weekend we would take turns in choosing a different takeaway, but it had to be from somewhere we had not tried before.

I ordered a keyboard from Amazon, yes that's right a keyboard. I'm currently working my way through an app called Simply Piano and I love it.

I have been learning a bit of Journey, 'Don't Stop Believing' and 'I've Had the Time of My Life' from Dirty Dancing.

My tonics have also been Sophie Ellis Bextor's kitchen disco to the point where I bought a bottle of gin with her face on it, and I love Stacey Solomon's Instagram stories.

Work has been hard and good in equal measure (work is as a Police call handler). Lockdown has affected many people in different ways, I am grateful to my work family for getting me through the tough shifts. I think between all of us we have completed Netflix and love a bit of a debrief on what we have watched after rest days. I still feel proud to serve the community that I live in.

I will be glad to see the images on the CCTV cameras of busy streets and people out having a good time.

Thank you NHS.

Thank you to the brave police officers and fire crews who face danger to keep us all safe.

Thank you to the amazing scientists who have produced the Covid vaccine.

Thank you to my friends who have checked in (you know who you are) I will never forget that.

Stay safe everyone, be kind, be happy. X

Sunday 2nd May 2021: Kirsty Jonas

As I sit here waiting for a beautician appointment it's hard to believe just how much can change in such a small amount of time! 35-year-old me had never heard of furlough and was always out and about, never at home. It would drive my other half crazy; he didn't understand my need to be out of the house every weekend. 35-year-old me would have never dreamt of home schooling, she wasn't a teacher, she wouldn't know where to begin………

March 2020: coronavirus was starting to gain media coverage and people were starting to wonder how much it would affect us. I vividly remember being called into a company meeting, to be told that starting from the following week we would work alternate weeks in the office. As I was allocated in the first group to work from home, I packed up my desk and casually said goodbye to friends and thought: 'It's only for a short while, we'll all be back together by the summer.' It never occurred to me, in this moment that I would be walking out on my employer's office of 17 years for the last time. In hindsight working for a live events company, I should have known life would never be the same from that point.

It didn't take long for the realisation hit, this wasn't going to be over by summer! We never did do alternative weeks in the office. I was at home with little work to do, as clients began putting work on hold and suddenly Boris Johnson was doing daily press briefings. It felt like overnight the schools were closed and we were no longer allowed to see loved ones. Panic and anxiety set in: 'I won't cope staying confined to our small house, I can't home school! I'm being furloughed, but I don't even know what 'being furloughed' is.' Once the initial panic wore off, I began to realise that whilst living during a pandemic was scary, my ancestors had lived through much worse. My family would still be together. We were not about to be separated due to war or a natural disaster. Life would be OK, and we would get through it together.

As the weeks went by, I realised I needed to appreciate the time I'd been given to spend with my 5-year daughter. Together we got into a daily routine of doing P.E with Joe, then we would do some home schooling before ending the day in the garden or out exploring close to the house for our daily exercise. It was incredible to discover we have a beautiful woodland nature reserve at the back of our home! Many evenings were spent video calling loved ones to talk and play games.

Sadly, it was not quite so relaxing for my partner who was working six days a week at our local supermarket.

The first lockdown came to an end, and our daughter returned to school. I began feeling lost and lonely as life appeared to be getting back on track to a certain degree for the rest of the family. However, it was becoming clear that live events were not going to be returning any time soon. At the time, furlough terms were changing and sadly I didn't expect it to be too long until redundancy loomed. In the past, I would have had panic attacks about losing my job – stressing over how we would afford to pay the bills, worrying that I would not got another job. Getting the call from work, oddly seemed to set me free. Suddenly I had the opportunity to do anything, and most importantly I got to have the whole of the school summer holiday with our daughter.

The summer was hot, and life had pretty much returned to normal, albeit I had no job. We spent so many days with friends and family – the children swimming in the sea, having picnics at the park, and visiting local tourist attractions. Life couldn't have been any better. Plus whilst enjoying a relaxing summer, I had been applying for new jobs and luckily it wasn't long until I received an offer of employment for a role which I love!

As 2021 approached, and it became clear, yet another lockdown was dawning. Anxiety started to set in again, could I home school with a busy full-time job? How long would this lockdown last?

Fortunately, I didn't need to worry, my new employer couldn't have been more understanding when it came to needing flexibility to home school. I won't lie, there were some really tough days and long hours but for the most part we cherished the extra time together again.

As we come out of lockdown again, I'm hopeful this will be the last one. I'm excited to see what the future holds and how we will all adapt to the new world.

This past 12 months has made me realise that change IS going to happen, and I can't control everything. Stressing and worrying about what will happen in the future will not help. Instead we should just enjoy the moment, although it seems tough, things do always work out!

I want to remember to appreciate the small things in life, being able to visit friends and family when we want, being able to just jump in the car and visit the beach. But mainly, that it is OK not to have every weekend planned out – to enjoy being at home!

Monday 3rd May 2021: Gill Lawson

May 3rd Bank Holiday Monday. I'm at home doing exactly the same thing as this time last year. Playing board games at home. But this year it is out of choice. The weather is forecast for double rain on the trusty Weather App so this is what we have chosen to do today. The shops are open, the beer gardens are open but I no longer feel the overwhelming urge to spend time outside of my home. This is major progress.

Of course, today is different from this time last year. I am happy to stay in because I have had a lovely, and normal-ish, weekend. I played netball on Friday followed by a delicious takeaway, had friends round in the garden on Saturday for a BBQ, and yesterday drove to York with my parents to meet my aunty and cousins. It was the first time my mum had seen her sister in a long time and it was so touching to see the joy in their faces. It being Britain, all of the above ended prematurely due to the shivering: our social lives are confined to the outdoors for now.

Before writing these reflections, I reflected on what I wrote last year. I was nervous about writing the first reflections due to fear of writing itself. I am not used to the freedom of writing and more comfortable with dreary reports. As it happens I absolutely loved it!

This time it was the fear of exposure. Not in a flashing the flesh way, but in a bare my soul way. A few weeks ago, after the long dark winter I honestly didn't think I would have anything positive to say at all. Each day was a struggle to get motivated. I reminded myself how lucky I was to have a job that I enjoy, great friends and family, and my health. I feel derisory saying it was just so tough.

Endless meetings. Nothing good ever comes out of looking at yourself in a camera all day. Nothing interesting ever happened on the 15-step commute to the 'office'.

So much and so little has happened in a year. After a premature and abrupt end to primary school our daughter has made the transition from a child into a young woman. Starting secondary school in the most unusual fashion where home learning, throat swabbing, masks, and bubbles are the norm. Secondary school really is a baptism of fire and I have to say Covid has sprinkled a welcome tad of water over the fire. Which is great.

I have missed my old life. But not all of it…the reset button has brought some welcome changes and I have enjoyed eating as a family each day rather than grabbing food on the way somewhere, and I have rediscovered my love of running – which my knees and jowls will not thank me for. I know who my true friends are and how amazing human beings can be. We invented and distributed a vaccine within a year. How impressive is that?

I love making plans. I love to feel excited about seeing people and places. It finally looks like some of those plans might actually happen. This year I hope to get some sunshine on my skin, camp, swim in the sea, drink cold beer from a glass and be reunited with my friends from home. One thing is for sure – it will be loud.

Tuesday 4th May 2021: Anna Franklin
When I read back on my original account that I wrote in April 2020, it's almost like another person is speaking. I was 37 days into self-isolation, desperately missing family, feeling incredibly anxious and work was petering out. Little did I, nor any of us, know what was still to come.

It is now 375 days later.

It has been a truly transformative year.

Of course, there have been moments and sometimes weeks when it has been incredibly hard. The hardest bit for me has been physical distance from family. I've wanted nothing more than to hug them. Especially grandparents, when it has at times felt like time has been stolen from us. But, overall, I've actually had a wonderful, life-changing year. I sometimes feel guilty for saying that. Guilty, because so many people have experienced loss, heartache and suffered tremendously. But I've also seen so much beauty throughout the year. So much has changed, some for the worst, but a lot for the better.

On a personal level, my relationships have strengthened. Lockdown gave me months at home with my husband-to-be, which is an opportunity we may not get again for many years. We enjoyed the simple things in life; the garden, quiet walks, shopping locally, board games and of course each other's company. I also had more time to ring my grandparents regularly, checking in with them almost daily. We had weekly Zoom quizzes with our parents and siblings (didn't we all?!). There was so much focus on making sure we stayed connected even when we had to be apart. I have always been a family girl, but boy did my appreciation for my loved ones grow even more. We became closer as a community and I'm pleased to say this has continued. We talk to each other on the street more, look out for each other and share things. Us friends sent each other care packages and notes, letting each other know we were thinking of each other. And I was also lucky enough to meet so many people online through my work, who have now become friends. My life is full of love and I couldn't ask for much more than that.

In terms of work, as I said, a year ago my business was fairly non-existent. But I used the time that we couldn't go anywhere or do anything, to learn and grow my skills to help me really build a heart-centred business. Since being diagnosed with chronic fatigue syndrome and fibromyalgia, I had been increasingly using energy healing and turning to spirituality to help me. Lockdown allowed me to explore this further and become qualified myself. I became a reiki master, a crystal healer, and an accredited life coach, amongst other things. I began using these things to help others. More and more I was recognising people in need of help for anxiety, depression, and a general pick-me-up and I was able to help them with this. Over the past few months 'Dragonfly Healing' has flourished. I've helped countless people get their lives back on track and now spend my days coaching and healing people who have been through similar struggles to me. It is incredibly rewarding to have a job that I've built myself from scratch and love, but also empowers other people to live a wonderful life too.

So when I look back, I realise that I've become much more content with life. The pandemic has really highlighted the things that are important in life: health, happiness, and love. But I've also become more ambitious; no longer waiting around to do the things I love – life is too short. I am stronger, happier, and healthier than I was before the pandemic and I think this is because it has taught a lot of us to slow down and focus on what is most important to us.

Looking forward, I dearly hope we keep this in our hearts as a reminder to appreciate the little things in life. To appreciate each other and the Earth we live on. To care for each other, protect each other and support each other. There are things to be grateful for all around us, if we just look. As I now write this, I can see a beautiful pure white feather floating gently down in the breeze outside. A poignant reminder, that when things slow down, it allows us to see the beauty in life.

It has been a time that I'm sure none of us will ever forget.

Wednesday 5th May 2021: Alix Young

When we first moved to King's Lynn, far away from friends and family, one of the first people I met gave me a great piece of advice. She told my husband and I that we needed to build our own family around us. This past year has shown me how true that is.

Neither of us are 'local' and our nearest family live at least two hours away. That distance has been fairly irrelevant when we can't meet at all – and video calls mean we probably speak more now than ever before. Face Time still isn't quite the same as meeting in person though – pre-schoolers don't really understand how phone cameras work! As various lockdowns eased over the past year the distance from family became more obvious, I can count on one hand the times we've been able to see those closest to us – my parents in law or my brother and his wife.

So we've taken that friend's advice and have built our own little family and friends network up here in Lynn though. They are a rather random mixture of people we've met through work, children, and the joys of the 'everyone knows everyone else' King's Lynn community. It's this family who've been our absolute rocks this year.

Firstly there's the mum I met through my eldest son's nursery pre-pandemic. Luckily our boys have started reception together and we were able to go to primary school inductions alongside each other and always had someone to discuss first day 'school mum' nerves with. She's been a huge support with helping to keep Charlie connected to other kids his age and never grumbles if the boys just end up fighting and/or crying within minutes of seeing each other as they struggle to adjust to socialising again. We've navigated the challenges of disrupted schooling, missed birthday parties and school gate friendships together.

There's also the neighbour I met shortly before lockdown who has become such a part of the family that she's effectively a surrogate grandmother to our two boys. She's been the most incredible support to me, especially as I lost both my parents in 2018. Whether it's borrowing her nearby garden to take the kids to for a 'day out', having someone to share in the boys' achievements or dramas or just a kind ear to listen to my moans and issues – she's done it all! I like to hope that my two boys being part of her life have helped her to get through this strange and unsettling time too.

Finally, there's the baby club group too. I was so lucky that my youngest had just turned one when the first lockdown started, meaning I'd had the chance to meet new mums and swap numbers already. This is something that so many parents have missed out on and something I never take for granted. Our little WhatsApp group has been a lifeline over the past 15 months. Two of the mums have had their second babies in that time and the others have been able to help and guide them through the trials and tribulations of juggling that second child with an energetic toddler. But mainly we've just shared little triumphs (like finding a long-forgotten chocolate bar in the cupboard) or milestones (like the first time you give up on potty training) in our own little WhatsApp bubble.

It was some of the mums from this group that I was able to see today, we haven't all been allowed to meet up since before the first lockdown so we are counting down the days to a proper night out for us all (babies very much excluded!).

It's all these people and more who've become my extra family – the ones I know I can share anything with and who won't judge me. Lockdowns and restrictions have separated us from so many but I count myself lucky that I've been able to build strong 'family' bonds with some new people too. I'm sure we would have built relationships had things been 'normal' but the events of 2020-21 have certainly made them even stronger.

All that being said, I do miss my actual family. Hopefully my parents in law will move closer later this year, and I can't wait to meet my new nephew when he's born in the summer. Perhaps top of my list though is seeing my grandfather when he celebrates his 101st birthday in June as we could only celebrate his centenary virtually last year!

Thursday 6th May 2021: Alma Sheren

This year has gone by in a blur. Normally we can recall the things we've done by pinpointing certain events and anchoring our recollections to those times to get our bearings, but as most interactions have occurred through a computer screen over the last year I feel I've lost my anchor a bit. Many of the things I thought happened last year actually happened two years ago!

This time last year, not a great deal had changed for me. I was already well used to remote working and juggling home schooling with my professional life, having done both out of necessity for several years, and if I'm completely honest, I've enjoyed much of the quiet and solitude overall. I think the hardest parts for myself and my son (who has high functioning autism) were the transition stages. The bits where we were coming in and out of lockdown affected us both, and me in particular much more than I expected. For the first time in years I started experiencing panic attacks and anxiety each time we came out of lockdown and I felt a strong and compelling need for assurance and certainty through those periods.

Thankfully, the places and people I work with have a high priority on mental health awareness and it's really cemented how important having a supportive work environment is, especially in times such as these. I felt comfortable speaking about the things I was experiencing, and just knowing it was acceptable to feel that way, and that there was support if I needed it made a big difference to how I felt overall.

The world didn't quite pause for me...

Surprisingly, I've been busier than ever over the past year, and my professional responsibilities and various projects have been steadily growing through the transitional lockdown periods, including becoming involved in an exciting leadership development programme with Greenacre Consult, Greenacre Group's new business division, which I've really enjoyed being a part of. But, whereas before I was working less hours but pulling myself in different directions at different times of the day and night, and often working weekends, I've streamlined my time and created the space I need to do things that are important in more structured segments. Mental wellbeing, family time, and work now have more balance and focus.

So what else is different from last year? Well, apart from the hair colour and things being a bit busier and more structured on the work front, not really that much. We are still lucky enough to be surrounded by beautiful countryside and manage to get out and explore in nature most days…my child is now man-sized, and it takes slightly more than a poker where the sun don't shine to get him up for the day and motivated, and the dog is still pup-sized (well OK, we've both grown sideways a bit…ahem) but we're all the same on the inside…just.

Being away from people that matter can take its toll, and one thing I am glad of is being able to finally catch up with friends and family face to face, in small portions, instead of relying on video calls. I've actually found myself wistfully looking forward to someone coming and jogging my beer as they clumsily dance past me with a cheesy grin on their face. I haven't had a good dance in a crowd for ages, and I'm guessing it's still a fair way off. But it's something to hold on to (the thought, and the beer, obviously).

Working smarter, balancing better and being more authentic

It's been really nice getting to know the people I work with on a more personal and human level, and seeing those relationships grow stronger and more supportive. It's made us sharper as a whole group, more resilient and more interactive with each other and those we communicate with. There has been a real drive in the housing industry to be more authentic and show our vulnerabilities, especially as leaders, so that the teams we lead can relate, feel supported and see that its ok not to be ok sometimes. The drive for more authentic leadership is helping to shape and modernise our future workspaces, and it's exciting to be a small part of that and to see it developing and the work environment transforming to prioritise the things that matter most.

Outside the workspace I feel more balanced too, and my evenings feel more like my own now. I've finished my work for the day, walked the dog, and as I sit here writing this, it's comforting to know that once the laptop lid clicks shut I will make myself a cuppa, put my feet up, snuggle up under a cosy blanket on the sofa with the pup (because where did that warm weather go?!) and switch off from work-related thoughts for the rest of the evening. My son has now finished his science project and is playing online with friends (still no change there!), and the long, golden shadows from the sun as it gently filters through the clouds tells me it is about to set, and the world is about to pause once more, for a short while, just until tomorrow, and I have a calm and peaceful sense that all is well.

Friday 7th May 2021: Steph Allen

It's fair to say that, for too many people, the ongoing lockdowns have been a time of sadness and pain. So, I almost feel guilty to say that I've enjoyed the last year! Please don't judge, but my work has always involved a lot of travelling and therefore I've always spent a disproportionate amount of time away from home; whether it's been long days or nights away on my own. I always thought I enjoyed that aspect of my work, but I've learned that I can be so much more effective without all the travel and have a much better quality of life! I'd been a Zoom user for a year or so before March 2020, so almost seamlessly transformed all my work onto that platform

Putting this in context, we no longer have close family, although we have godchildren (godadults, actually!) and lots of fabulous friends, so we haven't had to endure the pain of not being able to see elderly parents or grandchildren, although of course we miss seeing our godchildren and friends. We work together, each with our own clients so there's been a natural and welcome change to the tempo of the day! No early starts, no trains or flights, no late finishes! In reality, it means we've reduced the gross number of hours worked but have achieved so much more with our fabulous clients. On 'coaching days' we've often been able to start late and finish mid-afternoon and on 'workshop days' we haven't had to lengthen the day by travelling! Last week was a case in point – I was running a two-day workshop in Dublin! No travelling to Stansted, no check in queues! We joked that my check-in was 0925 – for a 0930 event! That's the key: 'we joked'! Laughter has always played a huge part in our life! Being able to spend more time together has given us more time to laugh! We're busier than ever, yet with more down time and a greater feeling of enjoying time together.

The extra time gave me the privilege of coaching a number of GPs in East London. I volunteered to support those who were struggling to balance the new ways of working with the appallingly high infection and death rates in East London. These inspiring women have been juggling home-schooling and home-life, with running their usual surgeries, mixing face-to-face with telephone and video consultations, as well as supporting the many families, who have tested positive for Covid. Some of their experiences were heartrending; many had contracted the disease and one, fourteen months on, is still unable to work due to diagnosed long-Covid. As with all my coaching experiences, I gained as much from my coachees as they gained from me; it's an honour to be part of their lives as they move through such life-changing experiences. One commented: *"I admit that I'm scared. I'll try not to let that show in front of patients and colleagues, but I won't be taking this 'on the chin.'"* Another said: *"We all need to keep our eyes open for colleagues who are struggling, and each of us is likely to need support in the months ahead. We'll also need laughs, virtual hugs, and coffee."* Hopefully real hugs will follow and 'my' GPs will build on their strengths.

Our life, therefore, moved into a different tempo with a gentle combination of paid work, pro-bono offerings, plus time for us. We've been able to think about how we can continue to support local businesses and new initiatives.

For example, being foodies and knowing that the hospitality sector would struggle, we made a resolution to support the amazing local restaurants which had diversified into 'dine at home' offers! Most weekends saw us taking collection of incredible menus from some of our favourite chefs and almost feeling we were eating out! It's great for us, but also I hope it creates a sustainable business model for those restaurants that might have struggled. This diversification has clearly worked as many aim to continue even when we are allowed to 'eat inside'.

Every business has had to change, whether it's GPs in East London, hospitality in East Anglia or the thousands of organisations, large and small that have created agile working options and, hopefully will retain the flexibility and choice that these bring. Yes, the last year has been tough for so many, but there are many gains that we would benefit from holding on to.

So what have I learnt?

- Work is what you do, not where you do it!
- Asking for help and supporting each other are vital.
- Each day is valuable - carpe diem!
- Laughter is key.
- Time together is invaluable.
- The tempo of our days can change naturally and it's good to just kick back and let that happen.
- Local businesses are innovative and, with support can successfully diversify and create new markets – there is a positive future out there!
- The inspiring 'The Boy, The Mole, The Fox And The Horse' has given me a life-message every day!
- Whilst I miss restaurants, theatres, holidays, and seeing friends, I am thankful we are all safe and well.
- Make up is vital regardless of where I am, but loungewear can successfully replace workwear!

Saturday 8th May 2021: Jacqueline Fry

Well, last year we sat in our front garden having our social distanced street party thinking it was novel and going to be short lived. Who would have thought 8th May 2021, I would have been grateful for a haircut on the 7th May, not having had one since December 2020.

The pandemic gave me chance to reflect on what was important and it opened up opportunities. I left my 14-year role in a housing association and stepped out of my comfort zone and into the world of the NHS. This has been very different to what I've ever experienced and has given me an insight into the way our health service is delivered. Bonus, I've had my jabs!!

My son was furloughed through both school shutdowns to parent/home school his son and as they both live with me that brought challenges around working from home but it also brought huge benefits. Not only did it give them time together that usually only goes to the mother during maternity leave, I have a long list of home improvements completed which he would never have had time to do on weekends where childcare is still the priority.

Not being able to spend time with my daughter has been hard, she also works for the NHS and has been busy with vaccination clinics. I'm truly proud of what she has achieved and been part of and there is still no end in sight. I'm sure we will be heading for boosters once the first and second rounds have been completed.

The first lockdown brought out community spirit, people laughing whilst waiting outside for prescription collection for those that were sheltering. Quiz nights online that went on for months. But sadly, this spirit doesn't seem to have continued, and opportunities to make changes in society appear to have been missed. I feel that the divide between the 'have and have nots' increased.

It's been hard for children, not least in missing out on time with friends to burn off energy and home learning, using technology.

Finally, normality is starting to return and yes, please keep it slow as we come out of this to ensure we don't have to do this again. A couple of weeks ago I managed to have a drink outside a pub with a friend, how nice that was to be able to socialise. And finally, I can see how much money I hadn't spent during lockdown through not being able to go out!

Sunday 9th May 2021: Thea Gant, aged 5
(as told verbatim to her mum)

When I stayed at home it was hard because I couldn't huggle my grandma and my grandad Basil and my grandad Chris and my nanna. That made me feel sad. It was hard because I couldn't come into Nanna's house and Grandad Chris' house and Grandma and Grandad's house. But now I nearly can. I have to do my distance still.

When I couldn't go with Mum to the shops it was very sad. Now I can. I went to the toy shop and I got some Lego. I love Lego now.

We had to stay at home because there was the bug. So the bug makes people sick. That's not good.

At home we did fun stuff like baking, we baked cakes and muffins. We played Barbies. We did tea together, sometimes. We went on the trampoline. When it snowed we played in the snow and we made snow angels and that was so cold. I roller skated outside but I fell over and hurt myself. But I'm getting good now. It's been very good being with Mum and Dad because I love them so much.

Homeschooling was weird and it was crazy. My dad was like funny as a teacher. I liked it because we all get along. I missed my friends because I love playing with them and playing games with them. I want people to be able to come to my house and do fun things like playing board games with my family.

It was good when I went back to school because I like to do Maths and PE at school. Teachers are very nice. And they teach us to work hard and they do some work for us to get us to be a grown-up. When I saw my friends again I was happy and I'll be happy when I see them tomorrow. I felt very happy to have school dinners again – like tuna and ham sandwiches and roast dinner.

People can come into the garden now – that's really good.

The jab makes you feel well and helps you to huggle your parents. I went with Mum when she got the jab and it was really sharp and she was fine. Dad hasn't had the jab yet because he wasn't old enough. I can't believe that because he's taller than Mum.

Today I have been pretending that it's Christmas Day. I made pretend presents and gave them out to everyone. Everyone was excited for pretend Christmas. Mum and Dad were laughing. I went to the park. I've been to the park a lot. My favourite things are the swings and the zip wire. I've also started playing tennis and it was really great and I loved it so much.

I'm looking forward to huggling Grandma and Grandad and Grandad and Nanna and everyone. When I can see everyone I'm going to play catch and I'm going to play bat and ball. Maybe I will have sleepovers. And maybe I will play board games with my aunties. I've missed everyone. So so so so so so so so so so so so so so much.

Monday 10th May 2021: Rosie Walden

Well, here it is, a little insight into lockdown life with a primary school teacher – half teaching from home and half in school – her husband, their two young children, and a sister-in-law. A few thoughts and feelings that I have had over the last 12 months, a completely mixed bag, and a whole lot of hectic-ness….well, sometimes!

Some days I feel like what has actually happened day-to-day in the last 12 months? Not a lot really, has it? Life has 'stopped', and then, I often think what HAS NOT happened in the last 12 months? Life has been BUSY, but busy suits my personality as I do not like to stop. I'm always, always on the go. I'm constantly trying to find 'new' and 'fun' things to do at home, or going on walks, trying to write exciting menus for the week ahead, and occasionally making time for me (I mean, this often meant doing a paint by numbers or completing my activity journal).

The hardest part though for me was trying to maintain relationships with the people in my life, when speaking to others: friends, family, colleagues, and pupils, it was via a phone and screen. The latter has been especially hard. I teach 5–6-year-olds. 25 absolutely smashing young people, to be exact, who in the last nine months I haven't actually seen that much face to face. Wild, right? And as for so many people, work has completely changed. I do not think, in fact I know, I was not prepared for how much my job would change and what it would look like during a lockdown, coupled with the feeling of urgency to try and be there for the young people. Was it possible to work harder and longer hours all whilst not seeing these 25 faces daily? Turns out yes, yes it was, and far harder than I or we (the education sector) could have expected. But it will always be worth it for the children we teach, always.

However what I was not prepared for was the toll it took on me. I am always an 'okay', 'fine' and or 'good' kind of person, that is just me. But much like anything in the last year, I was unsure, tired, anxious, and worried that I was not doing enough for my family, friends, and my class. Something I always feel is that I am not doing or being enough for those around me, but this took over, especially in regard to work. All this weighing heavy on my shoulders, as well as so many others too, and trying to make sure my husband, two small children and my sister-in-law who lived with us, were okay. It is only now that I have stopped and sat down to write this reflection, that all these memories, feelings and strong emotions are really becoming clear. Well, for the most part.

The school day, (I mean I had for a short time forgotten what that even looked or felt like), seemed so long ago and quite frankly the thought of having to be up and dressed like 'old times' was hard enough! However the 'typical school day' is something that my pupils and the staff in my school, and all schools, so desperately needed back, but we knew, like most others did, that it could not happen just yet. It was up to us as staff to support our children and their families in every and any way that we could. Trying to bring some normality back to these young people. I remember meeting after meeting to discuss where to start, what to try next, anything from a message on one of our online platforms, to a house visit, recording lessons, teaching live, food parcels, working within the community, preparing work packs for families and phone calls. Many, many phone calls. Hours each week calling families to say hello, checking in and offering any support that we could was a start and I believe now that this was one of the most valuable things that I/ we could offer given the circumstances at the time. Yet it still did not seem enough.

Then it was lessons. Oh my, how they were different. They went from being 15-40 minutes long in school to short, recorded lessons for children learning from home. These tended to be 2-10 minutes long and yet took considerably longer to plan, prepare, and film. As for filming them, well, I can smile at it now but my oh my, they took a while to get used to. Talk about being your own worst critic, but it did get easier, I got used to it. Although then I worried if it was good enough and what would others think as these were shared with lots of children. Some of our lessons were used in international schools, that took imposter syndrome to a whole new level for me. This was all whilst having to find a time to film these as my husband and sister-in-law were both working from home and having two, LOUD, small people running around too. One of those who needed home schooling too as she is in school herself and the other, well he is three, need I say more! That is just the tip of the iceberg into teaching through three lockdowns. A sentence I never thought that I would write but hey, here we are, and if I am honest, I enjoyed it for the most part. And would do it all over again for the young people!

Reading that back, it sounds, well I don't know, hard? Well I suppose it was, but actually, as clichéd as it sounds, I also really loved the time spent with my family. I also learnt a lot about myself too, even more clichéd, but it is true. I have learnt how I react to stress and how best to deal with it, mostly… We, as a family learnt to be creative, we made many changes to our house (that was super fun!), the children did loads of crafts and fun activities and most importantly, we created a greater bond, which is just gorgeous!

Tuesday 11th May 2021: Thomas Murray, aged 10 and a half

Lockdown was hard, especially in the winter. I didn't really enjoy home learning, I found it hard to get motivated. I much prefer learning at school where the teachers are always encouraging and make an effort to explain things. I missed my friends and talking to different people, I like sharing what I have learnt and what I have done. I realised how much I like school, it's great to be back!

Lockdown learning was nice for the flexibility and freestyling, I could do my work how I wanted and in a different way to how we might do it at school, like spend lots of time on drawing or writing. I still got it done but I did it my way. I also enjoyed some of the books that we read together as a class on Zoom, especially because my friend's mum had recorded some of the chapters. It was great to see her smiley face, their cats, and their house.

I missed being able to go out and away from where we live. The same walks around the village got boring and I'm looking forward to going to the pub for lunch! I missed seeing my friends and family at Christmas, I can't wait to see them this summer.

I did enjoy getting to know my mum, dad and brother even better. It was mostly good, but after a while some of their habits became really irritating! I also enjoyed the slower pace of life, and in the first lockdown it was good to get outside in the garden and do practical things. I learnt how to use tools with my dad.

I'm proud of my cycling, drawing, and writing – I did lots over lockdown and am now really good. They are all things that I want to keep doing more of too.

Now, I am looking forward to hearing less bad stuff on the news, and I hope that better action will be taken against climate change. It is one of the things that I became more aware of over lockdown, from listening to the news, reading The Week Junior and talking with my family and it is something that I care about a lot.

Wednesday 12th May 2021: Clive Bartlett
"Can you play Peppa Pig with me?"

[Sigh]. Gawd. Really? Does she not know? I'm 50 years old now!

But those eyes. Those, *"Pleeease will you play with me"*, toddler eyes. Who could refuse?

"Okaaaay. Go on then."

"Yayyy!"

I laugh – but just to myself. She's supposed to be poorly. And, come to think of it, I'm supposed to be working. But, if the simplest of things can give so much joy? Who am I to deny someone that moment – especially when that someone is my youngest?

With caffeine count at max and a newfound burst of energy, I'm ready to get stuck in. And drag this lockdown lump of a body around the floor until one of us gets bored. (I know who my money's on).

But hang on?

"Where's George?"

"Oh, he's missing – but that's OK."

OK? OK???? It most certainly is not O-bloody-K!!
This set cost 40 quid!!!

One year on from my first When The World Paused reflections – and it looks like we're well on track for returning to some form of normality!

"Tell you what? How about we go outside."

"Outside? Yaaaaay. I love outside."

And it's true, she does. Thankfully. It's far less stress on the knees!

For many reasons, over the past year, it's been hard to keep spirits up. But, as lockdown continues to lift, outside has rapidly become the most precious space of all. Both for myself and my kids.

We go for walks. Go to see the horses. We pick flowers. We laugh. Blow dandelions. We chat about anything and nothing. We skip. I trip over cracks in the pavement – and we laugh even more. Well, the kids do!!

And. It's. Awesome. No matter the weather.

Then there're the people we meet along the way. They smile. They nod. They mouth the words 'Thank You' as we all attempt to give two metres of space on a narrow country path…

"Well, she was a bit close!"

You can always rely on my eldest to tell it like it is. We take it to VAR. And both agree, it's got to be a yellow card.

But you know what? That's OK. Because it's the gesture that counts. The intention is there. The consideration. From both young and old. And it feels like the re-emergence of a long-lost community spirit that once reigned supreme. Although the piercing glare of an oncoming driver would suggest some bridges may take longer to build than others.

Briefly, I'm transported back to the late '70s. The back door of our house is wide open. And neighbours drop by with a "Cooooeeee. It's only me".

Happier times? Simpler times? I don't know. I was just a kid. But it feels like, back then, you didn't need a 'we're in this together' slogan for people to be considerate. Or want to help each other out. It was a given.

Maybe I'm wrong…

So, May 12th, 2021. A day, much like any other really – but with thoughts now turning to more positive times ahead. With playdates and clubs for the kids. Pub and Premier League football for me (get in, Norwich!). And a faint possibility of a family holiday – if we can find anywhere that isn't already booked out!

Ooooh, and it looks like we've got the green light for hugs outside of the family circle soon too. Although, for the life of me, I can't think who I'd want to go through that awkward experience with.

(That said, Kylie, if you're reading…)

However, amongst the happier thoughts of now, there is one thought that hangs over me. And it's this. If ever there was an opportunity for everyone (and by that, I mean the whole world) to come together for the greater good, then any point during the past 12 months was it.

Sadly though, I just don't think it's happened.

'I want to live in a perfect world, but that will never be,
Instead, I live in a world I made, learn to live with me.'

Wiz, Mega City Four

Thursday 13th May 2021: Janka Robinson

I have been thinking long and hard about all of our achievements during the past year, along with life's ups and downs during what seems like a never-ending pandemic. Work continues on from home. 2021's quarter one home schooling was interesting and thankfully, the kids have since returned to school – from trying to work full-time, this felt like winning a lottery ticket when the announcement came. Each day counts, although it can be nerve-wracking receiving a text message and dreading it's from school. When the kids were at home all of the time an uninterrupted cup of coffee was a luxury and why was it they were always hungry? I was constantly providing catering services!! My ideas of healthy snacks and lunches last year sometimes seem like a distance memory. I confess, it has been challenging not to see my family, virtual get togethers are simply not the same; as Ela (8 years) says: "it is weird we cannot kiss and hug them". I know very well what she means – it's been two years now since we last saw them. Sadly, we have experienced the loss of loved ones during this pandemic due to Covid and not being with family to provide our support and comfort has made it even tougher.

The four of us put together a bucket list and we will endeavour to complete everything on this list. We have done some of the simple ones, such as a meal at a nice restaurant, a return to team sport, even coffee and treats at Costa! However, it's the trips to see family that we are all looking forward to – the little ones are growing up so quickly.

How did we survive the second lockdown, nothing much has changed really! Plenty of coffee and cakes. More walks in the park and while out and about, taking in the surroundings a little more, which in normal circumstances might have gone unnoticed.

As for my girls, they think it is great that now Mummy can collect them from school as well as Daddy and being all together as a family unit has certainly made us closer.

However, despite all the plusses, sometimes, it feels like we're all on top of each other; the time together can sometimes be far from quality time. The demands of work and chores eat away at my time and it feels like there's no time left for me, at times we have been close to breaking point. Guess we just need a bit of downtime…

My hope is, that next time Michelle asks for my reflections, it will not be life during lockdown, but life after the lockdown…

Friday 14th May 2021: Caroline Fawcett

The language in my inner dialogue is still appalling, my children are still feral and my dog is incontinent but I couldn't be happier. I've remained a glass half full not half empty person through the pandemic – and usually a brim-full wine glass. While everyone else's life got smaller mine got a little bit bigger with a very special person coming into lockdown with us allowing me to carry on my work as a GP. Little did he know when he came to the Isle of Wight to visit in February 2020, with his overnight bag and two dogs, that he would never leave!!

Despite threatening to stop my personal blog, convincing myself that no one really wanted to hear my rantings on Facebook and my website, it seems my regular catastrophes were a source of entertainment and comfort for many that life was not as bad as mine – so on it goes!

We weren't long into the first lockdown last year when my entertainment bank was running on empty and I decided the only option was to call for a Christmas in April. Up went the Christmas tree with its beautifully handcrafted 'Boris Gabriel' from a paper plate on the top. It seemed appropriate to bring Christmas to an abrupt end a few weeks later when Boris was admitted to ITU with Covid.

Lockdown has mainly taught me that kids can't get through a day without bringing the topic of their bathroom accomplishments into at least one if not most conversations, and especially if I'm eating.

It seemed surviving lockdown was all about establishing rules:

1. Early on, any attempt to virtually try and take me around a Minecraft construction was prohibited.
2. My laptop is not to be used as a plate.
3. Pot noodles are not to eaten in the hot tub.

4. Cans of cider are not to be shotgunned in the bathroom.
5. After Millie the dog's emergency spinal decompression surgery in July, in a desperate attempt to enable her to walk again, the long-term double incontinence is regrettable but she was permitted one liquid and one solid accident a day. The nugget left for me in the pot pourri on the windowsill, although commendable for the agility and poise to get it there, was a deliberate breach of the rules and heralded a prompt removal to the garden to contemplate what she had done.
6. My son Zack was originally permitted one pointless question a day for me but when Alexa got fed up with him and refused to acknowledge anything falling out of his mouth, it seemed only fair to increase his quota to two with the second idiotic query to be reserved until I had a glass of wine in my hand. After questions such as when will he be old enough to use the word arse without getting told off and why we have toilets when you could just wee on the floor and wipe it up afterwards, I suggested we set up a daily half an hour Zoom question time with his granny instead.
7. My daughter Izzy's rule was to try and increase her step count in increments of five per day. She maxed out at 50 and reassumed her position mostly on the sofa and at the bottom of the international Fitbit steps league board.
8. My son Thomas was limited to only six excursions to the fridge in a 24-hour period in a vain attempt to conserve the last bit of pile in the carpet from the path he had carved from his bed to the fridge door.

My children devised an effective method for detecting a loss of smell in Covid and regularly farted on each other's heads to ensure their beloved siblings weren't exhibiting early symptoms.

Sadly, some of my patients weren't quite so self-sufficient. Never mind the biggest challenge to the NHS since World War II, the daft ailments and equally daft home remedies have flooded in. I've seen myself trying to convince a 64-year-old that it simply isn't possible for him to have growing pains, suggesting the medical breakthrough of lip balm to someone who had not considered it to manage their one day old chapped lips, and agreeing with a ninety year old, who still has not left the house in over a year but needs a little bit of moral support every now and again, that a nice hot cup of Horlicks should see her right. She's first on my list to hug when I can!

I went into lockdown with four of my best friends. I always had a close relationship with my children on the back of the adventures we've endured and this has grown through endless hours of laughter and silliness. We stayed safe but not sane. With my partner Jim, for some there might have been the option to come out of lockdown and decide not continue to live in each other's pockets, but for us there's nowhere we'd rather be.

Saturday 15th May 2021: Sarah Jones
Saturday 15th May 2021 vs. the last 12 months…

I'm writing my reflections on the same day as I did last year, when I was SO excited to be at work – the first day that the golf course at Barnham Broom reopened their doors after eight weeks of closure for a short lockdown period… little did we know!

We thought this was the first phase of returning to normal after what had felt like a lifetime, two whole months of not being able to go out. Two whole months of not being able to see people, to hug a friend or family member – we had to wear a mask to go to the supermarket!!!

Well, that's so funny looking back now – at how naive we were, how thoughtless we were, and how unprepared we were.

June brought us lots of sunshine and we were able to enjoy this at home and in the parks, I got an amazing suntan, I had fun in the sun with my bubble/support network and saw it as a little holiday at first. I thought wow, this isn't so bad, being paid through the job retention scheme whilst basking in the sunshine woo hoo.

July, although still lovely and hot, started to get boring, I missed the routine of work, something to focus on and feeling fulfilled. I HAD to do something, I needed a project and a routine. So, I started baking and cooking for people, doing pharmacy collections and deliveries for within my neighbourhood for those self-isolating (who had ever used that term before!?).

I started the 'Couch to 5K', this was great, I had an app that told me what to do as I went around the local roads and parks, I felt better in myself and I had a plan! Then I had a fall and banged my head, this meant the running had to stop. What now??

August – I found a buyer for my house and it was my birthday, boom! We were allowed to mix outside again so let's organise a big party, a chance to get together and see people we hadn't seen in sooooo long, a farewell party to the house. That was my focus for that month. I was also able to go back to work, part time on the flexi-furlough scheme 2.5 days a week. It was great, I loved it, August had to be my favourite month of 2020.

For the next couple of months I plodded along, doing my 2.5 days a week at work, seeming like I was making progress, booking people in for their Christmas parties – it was all going to be over and back to normal by December; Boris filled me with confidence and I wanted to believe so I did!

Bang, snapped out of it and back to reality as I am now having to call all these businesses and cancel their business events in November and Christmas parties in December. They cannot go ahead, we cannot celebrate Christmas and definitely will not be having the big New Year's Eve party I had dreamt of to say a big fat GOODBYE to 2020 and to Covid-19. It was still with us and not going anywhere, anytime soon.

As Christmas approached I was told that I was being put back on the job retention scheme, fully furloughed again, this time with no sunshine to give us the opportunity to get outdoors and enjoy the days. It was winter, it was cold, moody, and miserable. I tried not to think negatively about it, tried not to feel down… let's put a positive spin on this. So, some DIY started in the house again (now quite the handywoman, I will have you know).

I decided I wanted to read more, so I reached out on LinkedIn to ask for recommendations of some self-help books, I wanted to use this time to get in a better frame of mind, to be more positive, to better myself. A MUST READ – The Science of Self-Discipline (Peter Hollins).

I read this book and I genuinely feel like it was a life-changer for me, it changed my outlook, made me look at myself and make some adjustments. I changed my circles, in doing so I spent more time with those that are important and appreciated them more. I ate better (still am), drank less wine, exercised more (even if just walking) and now I can organise myself better. All of this equates to a happier, healthier body and mind.

In the last month I have taken up swimming for fitness and online fitness classes. I have had my very first golf lesson with the very talented Ellie at Barnham Broom and I plan to have more lessons, to take this up as a hobby and also for corporate golf events that I will be able to attend (plus I can have my lessons after work, super convenient, perks of the job!)

The biggy though, for me, is that I had my hair cut short!! I have had pretty much the same style hair since I was a teenager… I know, sad right! Long hair down my back, side parting always tucking it behind my ears. I am turning 40 this year and as part of the new, better me culture I am developing, it was time to grow up! I now have a long bob, just on my collarbone and I love it, why did I not see that I needed this before, the look is much more my age, more sophisticated (so I am told) and much more Sarah Jones, businesswoman as opposed to Sarah Jones, same as she always has been. I feel like a new woman in every way possible, try it ladies and gents, try learning to love yourself.

To close I should let you all know that I am now finishing my third self-help book and have my fourth ready to start. I am also going to re-read The Science of Self-Discipline, to re-fresh myself and give myself another kick-start as things really and truly, are now going back to normal – amen!

Sunday 16th May 2021: Samantha Slusar

How to sum up this last 13 months in just a few words? I think for me the overwhelming feeling is that of being trapped. I know, dramatic, right?

I'm a married 30-something with a husband who is also a 30-something. We have no children (by choice), and therefore enjoy a full social life. Unfortunately, we sadly lost our beloved dog at the ripe old age of 14 and a half last July.

We had always promised ourselves that after our dog had passed, we would make the most of being able to get out and see the world a bit more. Obviously, this virus had other ideas and stopped us in our tracks.

Anyone who knows us, will know that our sole reason for working as hard as we do is so we can spend those pennies on travelling. We will more often than not have some kind of trip booked, whether it's a last-minute weekend away or a couple of weeks city-hopping around Europe, we just love it. This was cut away from us on day one. Even today, we were meant to be in Spain. We are now in Cornwall.

Please don't get me wrong, I completely understand why, and you would think I would understand more due to my own family having a multitude of health issues. On the 30th of April 2021, it was the first time I saw my mum in person since before Mother's Day in 2020. This was mainly due to me being a key worker so still having to attend my work sites throughout the pandemic. So, it was too risky for me to see her before they have had their vaccines (which I'm pleased to say both my parents have had both doses now). It was certainly an emotional reunion, and so, so hard not to hug her so hard.

But even with all this, I cannot shrug the craving of a departure lounge. And I do realise how selfish that sounds when writing it down. But as my mum would say, "look at me, you don't know what's around the corner, so make the memories now."

We were much luckier than most last year and did manage a 10 day break in Turkey where we have friends who are just like family. We were so grateful for this time and the memories we made on that trip.

So what have I learnt from this past year? I'd like to say patience, but as I'm typing this I have another window open looking for flights at the end of the year. I guess what I've learned, is situations like this make you realise where you find your happiness, and that's ok in whatever form it takes.

Monday 17th May 2021: Anna Tydeman

When I look back over the year just gone I feel a mix of emotions. I am moved by people's acts of kindness towards one another, inspired by their resilience, thankful to the NHS and frontline workers and to everybody who made sacrifices for the good of others, and proud of us all.

My family and I have stayed healthy and seem to have weathered the storm: we're lucky compared to so many others and we do not take this for granted.

When I wrote my reflections for the first edition of When the World Paused last year, I had a lot of uncertainty and fear. Re-reading my entry, and those of the other contributors, it feels both a lifetime ago and like it was only yesterday. One of the things that strikes me most is how quickly we learned to live with the virus and the restrictions that came with it, not to mention those with school age children who had home-schooling to throw into the mix. Some businesses were forced to shut up shop for an unknown period of time, and those that could, moved entire workforces to living rooms and kitchens overnight. Remember those few weeks when loo rolls were flying off the supermarket shelves quicker than they could be restocked, and the big supermarket chains came together to try and restore some calm to their shoppers?

For me, life took an unexpected turn for the better and I have to pinch myself when I reflect on how much has changed for me in 12 months despite the awful circumstances which, in some ways, helped me get to where I am now. I'd left my job in March 2020, planning to have a few months break from work before finding a new job – a kind of sabbatical; I had plans of spending more time with my family, long beach walks, and finally learning how to use my fancy camera (which I've only ever used on the auto setting, and this is still the case a year later!) With the first lockdown being announced a week after I left my job, and fears about the economy and job market, I found it impossible not to dwell on the fact I wasn't working. For a while I was really worried about my future and questioned whether I'd made a bad choice.

During May, I had a catch up over Zoom with Michelle (the wonderful Michelle Gant, creator of When The World Paused). It was a social call but Michelle, whether she knew it or not, was the catalyst for me taking a different direction. She asked me what I wanted to do, and I shared that I'd long harboured a dream of being self-employed. Michelle's "you've got this" positivity and encouragement saw me leave the call with a plan. That same day I set about creating a website for my business which I launched at the end of May. I remember feeling overwhelmed by the support I received from my family, friends, and my network when I shared what I was doing – I had no idea that people would root for me as much as they did. That imposter syndrome I've nurtured for years seemed far away and I could not stop smiling that I was a step closer to achieving what had always seemed a bit of a pipedream.

There's a saying which I've always loved: *What if I fall? Oh, but my darling, what if you fly*' (Erin Hansen) and this was my mantra throughout those uncertain weeks when I wasn't sure I could make it happen.

Luck (and a strong network) seemed to be on my side, and I managed to sign my first clients in June. I was off, it was happening! I had a combination of retained clients and ad hoc work which suited me well, and as things have evolved, I've taken a part time employed position with one of my clients which gives me the stability and teamwork I found I missed, and the chance to work on other projects in my spare time.

So for me, the pandemic actually forced my hand in a good way when it came to my work. Had the world continued as normal, I would not have had that "I've got nothing to lose" perspective and I would have followed the plan, finding another full time employed position after my break.

It's been tough in other areas though; both my partner and I found the winter lockdown more difficult than we were prepared for. The weeks drifted into each other, with no clear definition between work and home, weekday, and weekend. We lacked motivation to do much of anything – I could look around the house and list a dozen jobs that needed doing but I couldn't be bothered to do any of them. The motivation to run the hoover round or wipe the bathroom sinks disappeared (not that I've ever been enthusiastic about these), nobody was going to see it so why bother?

We're lucky to live next door to some beautiful woodland, which is usually a place of calm and peace for us and our dog. During lockdown families descended into the woods to desperately try and burn some energy off their little ones and they weren't quite so peaceful, so we ended up going early or late in the day in order to avoid the crowds and let the dog run free. This meant we had long stretches of unbroken days at home to fill. I'd spend whole days buried in a book, until my eyes were strained, and then I'd move to Netflix in the evening. Our appetites changed and junk food was all we fancied, but thankfully McDonalds was open during this lockdown!

Looking at what I've just written, it would be fair to say we were suffering a kind of fatigue having endured so many months of pressure and uncertainty. Having chatted to others about it, I think many people felt this way, or a version of it at different points. I noticed a guilt associated with these feelings, after all, we were hearing heart-breaking tales every day of people losing their loved ones, or not being able to visit relatives in care homes so what did I have to feel gloomy about? I think the media and health experts on TV did a good job of normalising these feelings and this helped; it took away any pressure I might have felt to feel more upbeat at that time and I accepted it was just something to endure for a bit longer.

Let's hope this increased awareness and acceptance that our mental health has good and bad days, just like our physical selves, stays with us after the pandemic has passed.

Thankfully things improved during March. My parents received their first dose of the vaccine, the evenings started to draw out and the daffodils poked their heads out reminding us that winter would inevitably come to an end, and at last, the daily Coronavirus cases started to fall. The day the clocks changed on 29th March, the same day that it was OK to go and sit in my parents' garden and have a cup of tea, it was like a switch was flicked bringing positivity and promise of better days ahead.

With the end (almost) in sight, we found the motivation to get things done before Stuart returned to work and time was short again. He was like a man possessed, he painted the living room, re-did the front garden, planted hedging, pressure washed the patio, upcycled an old coffee table and gave the house a blooming good spring clean.

Oh, and I turned 40 – although I still feel as unprepared for adulthood as I did when I was 20 and I'm told that never changes. Unable to throw a party or go on an adventure to mark the day, I saw my family and friends individually which turned out to be lovely as I had proper quality time with them (and multiple cakes!) Stuart filled our living room with helium balloons while I was asleep, so in the morning I came downstairs to a full-on birthday carnival, and we had a special birthday tea. He did good! I couldn't have asked for more and I smiled all day, if I had another 40th birthday I'd choose to spend it exactly like that.

As I sit here now, we can visit pubs again. I'm not quite ready for pubs yet, but yesterday I popped into town for a browse round the shops and it was wonderful – as anxious as I might feel about leaving the safety of my home, it reminded me that

I'm pretty resilient and this although this year will leave a lasting memory, we'll come out the other side of it.

Tuesday 18th May 2021: Charlotte Sexton

I keep finding that it's pretty unbelievable that here we are one year on from when I sat to write last time and the world is still not actually that much different. Two further lockdowns since, and we are now starting to see a glimmer of hope on the horizon with restrictions lessening and the vaccine having the positive outcome that we had all hoped it would have.

Upon reflection, the days feel to me to have been lengthy, attempting to fill them with activities to numb the monotony - but the year has passed as fast as a rocket!

My children, now aged 9 and 10, have grown in height and around the middle! At the start of the first – supposedly three weeks of lockdown/school closure – I got out ingredients to make us a special treat of homemade pancakes for breakfast, slathered with chocolate spread and sugar of course. Little did I know that one year on and my kids would still be expecting this breakfast ritual to take place every morning in my kitchen prior to the commencement of daily home schooling. I must have easily made about 2,000 pancakes over the past year. Pancakes will always remind me of my children in lockdown…I think both of them are now skilled pancake makers themselves, which will be a handy tool to have later in life to impress their housemates at university during a hungover and hungry morning maybe! They expected the pancake making to continue when they eventually went back to school, but I had to draw a line at that and they are now reserved for weekends only.

I actually felt sad when home-schooling came to an end. At first I found it so hard trying to juggle two different stages of schoolwork and working from home myself. The second school closures were easier though and much more fun for the children with the introduction of Google Classroom and live Zoom lessons. After numerous technical hiccups from both the parents and the teachers I really got to grips with the Zoom lessons which were a godsend at allowing me to crack on with my own workload. The familiar sounds and sights of their teachers live in my kitchen and lounge respectively (one child in each room) every day. My daughter's lessons seemed much more 'fun' and by the end of the term I felt that I had subconsciously learned everything there is to know about Ancient Egypt that I'm sure I could pass an A'level on the subject.

They have been back at school a few months now and this now feels like a distant memory, but a time that I will cherish and a feeling of pride with being responsible for a small part of my children's education, I hope they have fond memories too.

Looking to the future I had my vaccine last week. It did feel surreal sitting in the waiting room. I felt like I was in some kind of military precision operation and I was impressed with the friendly and efficient nature of all of the volunteers and medical professionals involved. It felt like a big force for good and I must admit that I did feel unexpectedly emotional.

Just yesterday we entered the latest and most significant lifting of restrictions so far since the pandemic began. We are now officially allowed to hug friends and family from outside of our household for the first time. However, plans to ease restrictions completely next month are currently in doubt due to mutating virus variants and even sub-variants, threatening our complete future freedoms at this point in time. There may always be variants as with any virus, but I hope that in time we will be able to live amongst this, with the vaccine doing its job.

As usual I will hope for the best and stick to my motto in life which is 'keep on putting one foot in from of the other'.

Wednesday 19th May 2021: Jodi Coathup

A year on from my last post and everything seems different but strangely similar. The darkness and fear of Covid has definitely gone but the uncertainty lingers on. We can now hug, drink inside a café and pub but the spontaneity of it all still seems to be missing and I sort of worry that maybe it's gone forever.

I'm not a planner by nature, I'm much more of a last-minute type. But to avoid any further disappointment for the children, I've been on a booking mission: cinema, bowling, trampolining, sleepovers, days out… All the things that the children say they've missed. My calendar is now bursting at the seams with excitement and a nervous anticipation – what about if these activities don't live up to the hype? What about if it's too busy? What if I forget to wear my mask?

I had to flick through the photos on my phone to just remind myself of things we did during a year of lockdowns, opening ups, and all things in between. I was pleased to be reminded of some of the smaller pleasures in life; a paddle in the sea, sweet peas from the garden, cooking with the kids, camping in Norfolk. Of course, there are many things I didn't capture such as: the epic fail of home learning during the spring term (I should point out I am a teacher but my skills were very much redundant at home!), the weird underground world thing where only certain professions were allowed to go into their places of work, the 20 days of isolation while fighting off Covid, the death of my 97-year-old Nan from Covid, the tears of my children struggling with the disruption to their normal routines. All in all it was a bit of a mix 'n' match year, but we've survived and possibly come out the other end slightly better humans.

I had my first Covid jab just the other day. Thankfully that has been my only experience of the NHS during this time. What a fantastic service! I booked the night before, rocked up, and was in and out within 10mins. It's phenomenal to think what has been achieved and how amazing our country and the people in it are. We've risen to the challenge of fighting this pandemic – what a time to be alive!

As a teacher I've been lucky enough to work throughout the pandemic. The children have shown such strength of character to deal with the changes and take it all in their stride. My school has always been good at addressing children's wellbeing and mental health, but the pandemic has brought about a new approach to teaching and learning, well, in my class anyway. The pace that we raced through the curriculum before now seems so pointless. The pandemic has given me the permission to really respond to my class as individuals. We've had days when children just need a bit of down time, time to talk, time to share, time to just be, without the pressure of having to write it down. Our children are smarter than ever because they have such a high degree of emotional intelligence. They can give themselves permission to express themselves in ways that suit them, they've been given the vocabulary to talk about how they are feeling and all within a nurturing and caring environment. As a profession, I really hope we can keep the wellbeing and mental health side of the curriculum at the forefront of what school is about and let that lead our learning.

My final thought is about reflecting on my reflections in last year's When The World Paused where I used an analogy of a fairground and I think it still stands. I'm still on the rollercoaster, but I've got used to the ups and downs of it, parts of it are even enjoyable. I think once the warmer weather makes an appearance and I can kick off my mask, I might even treat myself to a bag of candyfloss –without having to pre-book!

Thursday 20th May 2021: Johnny Wharton

Lockdown came a bit like a tsunami, a small ripple followed by a forceful steady surge of disbelief, denial, and information overload. From my selfish point of view, I relished the chance to cancel work: being self-employed with absolutely no guilty consequences, as Boris Johnson had told me that is what we must do. A stunningly beautiful spring meant a lot of outside living, really taking notice of the changing spring, all on our own doorstep: walking in the village on footpaths which I had taken for granted, preferring those further afield.

As weeks rolled on, normality in the form of my work gradually crept back in and was welcomed.

Driving around the quiet village roads, talking to my customers - usually about Covid and the latest news on Covid - waking in the night, worrying about passing on Covid to everyone I met.

Ironically, I was able to meet and go into customers' houses to work, but I was not able to see my children, grandchildren, or friends.

Visits to my frail mum in her residential care home understandably came to a sudden stop. This happened to so many other families. We never knew how much Mum was aware of what was going on in our world and we didn't know what was going on in her thoughts. Meeting up with my brothers in Mum's company every Sunday stopped. All care homes were given instructions to only allow one designated visitor: that role was mine, but not being allowed to go inside. All home visits were done through her open window: standing at Mum's open window hoping she knew who I was and why I wasn't inside with her, holding a mobile phone up to her so my brothers could speak to her, trying to keep some sort of contact up between us all. Paranoid about even passing a simple bunch of flowers into the home in case Covid should follow in.

Little did I realise how long this would last and that there would be no more holding of her hand until the last few days of her life.

We are now coming out of lockdown. How exciting! We are off on a big journey outside the county of Norfolk, wow! Heading off to see our daughter, having not seen her for nine months, and having missed her so much. We shall make sure we will visit her much more often in the future.

We have just had a proper birthday tea with one of the grandchildren, so different from his last birthday as that was done on FaceTime, so good to feel his excitement with his special day. He went to bed and was upset because he wanted his birthday back.

Heading off to visit favourite coffee shops – what a luxury to look out over the sea while tucking into jam and cream scones.

The confidence we now have because we've been given the vaccination is lovely, we just cannot wait for our children to be given inoculations.

I am not thinking of holidays yet which is unusual, I am always ready to travel somewhere. I think it's because we are making decisions about downsizing our home and cutting back on work which was always a part of my social life. Moving from a house/home where we spent so many years – all our children were brought up here – but all have finally moved out.

Lockdown has shown me how much I enjoy just walking in the countryside, time in the garden, and the simple pleasures of just popping in and seeing people. I cannot believe how much this decision process – of cutting back on work and downsizing – has unsettled me and I do wonder if we had not had lockdown,

I would even have given it a second thought and carried on as usual.

Friday 21st May 2021: Claire Smith
Balance… but not as we know it.

What a difference a year makes. I have just reflected on my reflections from a year ago and how my life has changed. I said I didn't want to return to my old life and I haven't.

This time last year, I was on furlough worrying about being made redundant, experiencing a whole range of emotions, and wondering what was going to happen. I was feeling overwhelmed. I was checking social media far too much, I was trying (and failing, often) to create a routine and I was really missing my family and my friends.

So, what has happened in the last 12 months? Like so many other people I have attended countless Zoom quizzes but also enjoyed online wine tasting, a virtual cooking class, and drag queen bingo! I have continued to spend time getting out of the house, exploring lovely Chester where I live and new walks round Cheshire. Oh, and I have an actual boyfriend. Hurrah.

I have learnt to bake scones and lemon drizzle cake – it is ok if it isn't perfect! I have continued to read which I love; I keep a journal (great for putting down how I am feeling and what I am grateful for). I even have eggs delivered from my neighbour in the village. Who even am I?!

Was I made redundant – yes I was. That was a bit rubbish. In hindsight – I was running myself ragged and I look back now and realise I don't need to be such the workaholic anymore. I had never been made redundant before and it is harder than you realise to process the emotions. The pandemic has impacted people in many different ways and being a positive person certainly helped me get through. Friends and family rallied round (virtually of course). You really do learn who your true pals are.

The world pausing caused me to stop. For me that was a good thing.

So… did I manage to secure a new job… yes I did and I love it. Plus I get to work with one of my best pals every day! I have the chance to really be me. I feel valued and appreciated and the confidence to use my voice and not slip back into my old ways of saying yes to everything.

I really cannot wait to spend more time with my family and friends. I had a birthday lunch with my sister last week. It was wonderful. I look forward to buying my nephew Freddie an ice-cream! Plan a social life, go on lots of dates with Jamie and invest in myself. Take it back to basics and enjoy the simplest things. Today I am sitting in my sparkly new home office, tapping away, smiling to myself. It has been a good year. I am lucky. My friends and family are healthy. I am healthy. Have I achieved the balance I talked about a year ago? Not quite. Am I in a better place than I was – absolutely.

It is only seven weeks until I get to be with the girls aka The Sisters. A weekend away. One that we thought would never come round. There will be hugs and laughter and the odd tear I am sure as we celebrate friendship and missing one another.

I am still trying to achieve that balance between me, work, friends, fitness, and family. The difference now - I have slowed down. I don't feel guilty, I feel content. I have a greater sense of calm, I'm happier and for that I am grateful.

Saturday 22nd May 2021: Jayne McGurk

What a year it has been. The last time I shared my reflections on When The World Paused, a year ago, everything felt so much more positive; even after the rollercoaster ride that Covid-19 brought… last time felt very different.

As I sit typing this, looking out of the window at the pouring rain, I remember back to last summertime and the weather was glorious… we were coming out of lockdown and everyone felt much more positive; we all had hoped that we were over the worst and the only way was up. Little did we know what lay ahead. I wish I could sound more positive about these past few months but I think that Covid has just zapped energy and at times some positivity from me. We dare not build our hopes up any more about holidays, family times, even the thought of no more home schooling… just in case.

My youngest daughter started at the comprehensive school in September. No transition meetings, no party bus or Leavers' Mass, no school trips and summer fun to mark the end of her primary school years and this felt very sad. However, off she went, with all of the other children; back to school with lots of catching up to do and definitely no more lockdowns… and luckily that was the case for both of my girls at comprehensive school. They did see the autumn term through without any Covid related time off, although this did feel like an accomplishment in itself, especially as most of their friends seemed to have to take periods of self-isolation. Primary schools however, not so good. I'm a primary school teacher and my year group bubble isolated twice; all very stressful, last minute, causing a ruckus with parents pointing the finger of blame for another closure. My niece had to take three quarantines, missing almost a whole half term away from school before Christmas. At just 7 years old, she wasn't sleeping and suffering such anxiety each time when she needed to return to school… all so very sad but understandable.

And that brings me onto Christmas. Boris was determined not to cancel Christmas, but Covid had other plans. Our little Reception children didn't manage to film all of their Nativity play pieces that we'd intended sending home as parents couldn't come in to watch. We closed last minute after another positive case in our year group bubble and it was all so hurried that their Christmas cards and gifts all sat in the classroom untouched as they all went home. We consoled ourselves with the fact that they would soon return in early January but it wasn't to be.

Should the grandparents come for Christmas lunch? Shouldn't they? Maybe better not, just in case… but wouldn't it be lovely and the turkey is HUGE. Anyhow, after much umming and ahh-ing it was a very last-minute NO. No search for Santa Claus on Christmas Eve with the family and all of the children… the pantomime was on and then off, and then back on and then off again! Christmas Mass was still running but trying to book a space was almost mission impossible. Anyhow, we managed to get booked so mask wearing but without any Christmas carols we were so delighted to be able to enjoy something of our usual Christmas traditions. And Santa Claus did still manage to make it and the girls left him some hand sanitiser out, along with the usual carrots and mince pies. The tier system put a stop to even the most low-key New Year's Eve celebrations, so another Zoom party with friends it was… some not so great behaviours from the tween-agers…. Happy. New. Year.

Lockdown no. 34567910…… No school for the girls but I must still go into work and no they cannot come into school with me this time to protect the bubble; husband is away working on the ship and Grandma has not had her Covid jab yet = STRESS! Thanks to my boss for allowing me to work a slightly shortened day, however left unattended to home school, the girls did manage to block the toilet (not so bad) and try to unblock it (BAD. Very bad…) along with many other faux pas that I would rather forget all about.

And so here we are. Another very wet and cold day in May. At least we can now head indoors to eat and drink and be merry again. The girls have headed to see Peter Rabbit – their first film at the cinema in a very long time, followed by lunch 'out out' too. WOW. Is this really it….?

Sunday 23rd May 2021: Julie Shield

As I re-read my reflections from the same day in May 2020, and start to write this in May 2021, I could never have imagined that the pandemic would still be a big part of our lives. Had we known, I don't think we would have been able to cope with what lay before us – the uncertainty, fear, anger, sadness, and downright boredom at times has been up and down like a rollercoaster! Yet, here I am, still working from home, still wearing a mask, and still not able to travel freely. I have not seen my family in over 18 months (us in Amsterdam, my family back in the UK) and with no firm plans in place, we are not quite sure when it will happen – but the vaccine brings hope that surely it can't be too long!

The last year, although difficult, has not been traumatic. Our family and friends have not been seriously ill and no close family has caught Covid (or if they did, they did not present with symptoms). I feel like one of the lucky ones, because like all of us, I have seen the media coverage, heard stories from other friends, and as the virus continues to spread, the news shows us the devastation in India and Brazil that people are dealing with.

With feeling lucky, comes feeling guilty. My husband and I are both working and our jobs were never in doubt, we just learned how to work in a virtual way. My kids, although a bit annoyed at what was going on, have remained happy and healthy and adapted well. Why the guilt? I think I feel a bit helpless, unable to really do anything other than obey the rules, bloody confusing as they have been!

Reflecting back on the last 12 months, I can see some positives. We're still cycling – me and my lovely ladies (The Fairy Bikers) are mad keen cyclists now and have more kit and apps then we could have ever imagined. In the last 12 months I've cycled over 3000km and laughed and cried my way through them. They are a great source of comfort for me as we talk about anything and everything whilst speeding through villages and towns of the Netherlands that I never knew existed.

Sadly, our planned charity cycle ride from London to Amsterdam got postponed from June 2021 to June 2022. That was a bit of a blow as this goal was our momentum to keep training when we really didn't feel like it. The good news is we were able to transfer to another cycle of similar distance and move our sponsorship money with us so we are still supporting three amazing women's cancer charities. In September, we'll be cycling from Milan to Venice and today we even felt confident enough to book flights as we feel it will likely go ahead. But who knows what the next few weeks and months hold for us all with Covid still very much with us.

Another positive is running and swimming – it's now something I love to do and if you had told me that 12 months ago, I would not have imagined I'd actively look forward to running after a day at the laptop. It really has kept me sane when it felt like that was the only 'thing' we could go out and do. I'm no athlete, and any hope of becoming one is well and truly 30 years too late, but just knowing I can do it has brought me happiness. I still dream of doing a triathlon, beginner level of course, so maybe it might happen if I keep at it long enough.

My overwhelming positive has been friendship. My friends are just amazing, both here in the Netherlands and back in the UK, friendship has been something I have truly valued. Letters, cards, even WhatsApp messages from those who care about me and my family have made those difficult days easier and made me feel that none of us are alone in this battle with a virus that has kept us grounded and restricted in a way we have never experienced.

Lastly, I am truly thankful that both my parents and grandma are fully vaccinated so I can stop worrying about them (well, less than I was before they had it!). This time last year, my grandma had been taken into hospital and I was really worried about her, but I'm happy to say she's still doing well – and enjoying her glasses of red wine when the mood takes her. Thank God for FaceTime so we can feel connected across the North Sea.

Let's hope the next 12 months are less eventful – what with Covid, the changes for us as Brits in Europe, and the utter failure of the UK entry in Eurovision last night, things can only get better – right?!

Monday 24th May 2021: Fiona Buchan

'When the World Paused'…, strangely, despite life slowly opening back up, this seems more apt now than it did a year ago. Time doesn't make sense anymore. It seems like a lifetime ago I sat down to write last year. Perhaps this is because none of us are the same people now that we were then. Our journey as both a family and as individuals at first went unnoticed. We considered ourselves lucky. We had a house with space for everyone, a garden to escape to, family close by, wonderful friends, no financial worries and we were all in good health. Even when Adrian was made redundant in June we counted our blessings as we had savings to fall back on and I for one celebrated the opening of 'School of Daddy'. Despite not seeing family in person at Christmas, Zoom calls seemed to add an exciting dimension to the day and I revelled in the scaled back 'it's just the five of us' approach to festivities.

However, I hadn't appreciated the toll this restricted way of living was taking on us all. In October when our daughter began getting into trouble at school I didn't see her and echoed the disappointment of her teachers. It wasn't until a couple of weeks later that I paused, lifted my head out of my workload and looked at her. This wasn't who she was. What was going on? She has always had an inner strength I've envied. She is incredibly shy and doesn't seek the limelight but she has courage and determination that enable her to navigate most situations. It hadn't occurred to me that she would struggle with the transition to secondary school. She hadn't been put in a class with her close friends but this didn't worry her. She liked meeting new people and was looking forward to the independence of 'big school'.

Why hadn't I seen the signs earlier? There hadn't been a transition. There couldn't be; the schools were shut. How was she supposed to make new friends? They weren't allowed to chat in class. They couldn't meet up after school or invite friends back for tea. They weren't moving about the school from lesson to lesson staying instead in mixed ability tutor groups where the role of the teacher often had to focus on discipline. It just didn't make any sense to her. She couldn't find a way to fit in and I almost missed it. Thankfully, I didn't miss it and she now knows that we will always be on her side. As soon as I contacted her teacher, support was put in place and she began to turn a corner – right into another school closure.

There is no doubt that the third lockdown changed us all. Adrian, after six months of coming a tantalising close 'we were splitting hairs' second, started a new job. A good thing. This meant that 'School of Daddy' was replaced with the less organised 'School of Mummy'. Not a good thing. As our youngest said when the schools did reopen: "At least our teachers know what they are doing!" Children aren't meant to be isolated. Children aren't meant to think that there is illness in the air and I am definitely not meant to home school while home working. My benchmark for a successful day became getting them to clean their teeth! There were however pockets of joy. Sledging at lunchtime sticks out.

I let myself believe that everything would be ok when the schools reopened. I'd be able to get my work done and not feel like I was neglecting the kids. The children would finally be able to see their friends and enjoy school life. Adrian was working again, vaccinations were being administered at warp speed. We would all be ok. We were not all ok. All three children began showing signs of real anxiety, I burnt out and, for the first time ever, was signed off work for a while. Oddly, Adrian, who had endured six long months of job hunting, seems to have fared the best.

We are all gradually, with help, getting back on our feet. I have returned to work, Gracie, who I am so incredibly proud of, is beginning to sparkle again. Daniel has embraced the help given to him by the school, has shown that he has real depth and has taught us all a few things about good mental health. Lucas began to thrive once activities reopened and has us ferrying him to numerous sporting events each week, all of which he throws himself into. The little boy who once wouldn't leave my side is now standing tall.

The pandemic has taught me valuable lessons. Despite everything I am calmer. As life speeds back up I no longer move too quickly to appreciate the moment. Our family is held together by a strength I hadn't noticed before. When the arguments subside, and eventually they do, we listen to each other. We have genuine shared interests that can, with varying degrees of success, distract the kids away from their online worlds for a bit. We seem to have more respect for each other than we did a year ago – although this is well hidden at times! We have spent so much time together and experienced this rollercoaster together that, without any of us noticing, we all feel closer. We know what is important now. I don't think we did before.

Tuesday 25th May 2021: Jo Lake
LOCKDOWN

Wow, how scary was this when we first heard it. I was at work and they were talking about the schools closing like they were in Scotland. I was given a letter from my work telling whoever stopped me on my journey that I was a keyworker (I'm a personal banker) and needed to be travelling. Every day at 4pm (or was it 5pm?) I would switch on BBC1 to watch Boris tell us our lives were in danger and we needed to protect the old and vulnerable. I was terrified.

I lost my mum in 1994 and my dad in 2014 and for the first time ever….I was grateful for this. They would never have coped with lockdown or face masks or Tesco running out of toilet paper. I could barely cope at the beginning. Then, when I thought I had made my last pasta bake ever, home schooling hit! Trying to book my in-laws a slot with a supermarket at midnight so they could isolate and having to wait half an hour to even get on the site. The world was going mad. Then pasta flour and toilet paper slowly started coming back. I forgot to watch Boris one evening and the world didn't end.

The deaths started to drop and no-one in my family had had IT….that thing that just hung over us…it was a black heavy thing that scared me silly. But I hadn't died, my husband hadn't or my son. I had grown my own flowers for my hanging baskets and discovered Amazon had everything I needed. I had saved a fortune in having my nails done and bought some garden furniture with the money. I had survived without pasta and hadn't run out of toilet paper. It wasn't so black or heavy anymore. I wasn't so scared. Then lockdown ended and we had summer.

Not quite a normal summer but we could see friends and family, even if it was only through glass. I enjoyed not going to Tesco every day to buy things I didn't need. I didn't have a cold. We were the healthiest we had ever been and it was warm, and sunny, and the deaths were still dropping. Maybe it would disappear they said, just like the flu they said. Then it didn't and autumn came.

Lockdown two or was it the tiers? I can't remember which came first but it didn't matter because we were happy in our little bubble. We both still worked normally and home schooling was a thing of the past. Masks and hand sanitiser were a thing of the present but it wasn't as scary as before. Until the death certificates started coming in at work and I saw real people in front of me who had lost their mum or dad or husband or brother. Then it wasn't scary. It was sad, very sad. I was sad and a bit angry if I am honest. All those people saying it was fake news and no need for lockdowns or masks and it was a crime against our civil rights. When all I was seeing were sad relatives or angry ones, or those that had just accepted it but had no light in their eyes. Then someone mentioned a vaccine and a whole other set of emotions appeared.

Then we lose the land for our farm (I also have a farm with my husband). Then that is all that matters. Christmas can sod off…we can't see anyone anyway. Covid. Yes that black heavy thing. It is just something we are living with. We need to try to save our livelihood….without moving a hundred miles away. Without leaving our elderly in-laws or changing schools. Something is heavier and scarier that Covid.

Lockdown three……it's a breeze. Home schooling, pah….we have got it covered. Plenty of stuff in the shops and I have got this slot booking thing down to a T. I may have even found land for the farm…..MAY!!

Then my husband gets ill….very ill and it's not Covid. But I can't see him because of Covid….even though I have had the jab. He needs a big op. But I still can't see him. My son is scared, I am scared but we still can't see him. Then he comes home. Different. Thinner, older, different.

Vaccinations, Covid, and farms - they don't matter anymore. We just need him well. Then he has to go back in….another operation maybe, but we still can't see him. I hate Covid now…..it doesn't scare me…..it doesn't make me sad……I hate it. But the vaccinations are working, the numbers are coming down. But it will never go away. So I hate it.

I loved lockdown, saved money, spent more time with my son, learned gardening, exercised with my friend…..no pressures of dressing up and putting makeup on. I loved it. But I hate Covid….hate it.

Wednesday 26th May 2021: Stephani Davis

I didn't take part in the 'When The World Paused' journal last year, I wanted to, but I was not able to put what was occurring into words that would make any sense to anyone. I found I needed all my energy to adapt to what was happening.

I gave a lot of thought about what I would write and why I was doing it, and I decided to focus on some of the things I learnt and positive things to come out of this unique year as they can easily get forgotten and I don't want to forget them.

I love to learn. I can't get enough of it although I feel like I retain information for less time as I get older. When lockdown started, I knew I would have many feelings, but I never considered how much I would learn about myself over the year. I thought being in my forties, I had myself mostly figured out, but the year taught me that as with any new experience comes new insight and what you think you know can change.

I learnt about sacrifice and being part of it with the nation, giving up doing the things that are important to us – and that sometimes we take for granted – to help keep everyone safe. I didn't feel I had ever experienced anything on this scale before. I love spending time at home and am happy pottering around, so I didn't think I would struggle with being indoors. It's interesting how things feel different when freedom and choice are taken away. It seemed to give a new meaning to 'save it for a rainy day'. I would love to say I cleaned out cupboards or finally read all the books I had been wanting to get through, but March to September feels like a bit of a blur and I am not sure what I did to occupy myself; my only memories are building Lego and gardening.

Sometimes I found the things which I did regularly even before lockdown became harder to achieve and required more focus. On three occasions my supermarket delivery turned up containing two or three items; pop tarts and milk became a routine weekly shop. On another occasion, when I did manage to checkout my online shop properly, I was awoken one morning at 6am to a food delivery on my doorstep – who knew you could get a delivery at that time… from that day on when I selected what I thought was 6pm, I double checked the time slot.

I learnt a lot about relationships during the year. I have a strong relationship with my son, he is my everything. We spend all our time together when we are not at work and school so I didn't feel lockdown would affect us. I guess I was naive to think that when my role suddenly changed, and I was supposed to be both mum and teacher. Luckily, we both realised early on that teaching was not a career option for me and we found our own way to ensure our relationship as mum and son was the priority and education had to fit in around that.

My work is important to me, I am lucky to have a job I love and even though I already had all the equipment to work from home, it was of course a massive change not to see people every day. I felt lucky to adjust quickly and enjoy working from home, finally having a purpose for the kitchen table other than a collection point for any item that ends up on it. I was surprised to find that I never felt alone, every day I felt part of the same team as before. I know this was a result of having a caring and supportive employer and amazing colleagues. I want them all to know how grateful I am to them for their energy and support during the year.

I realised how lucky I was to have a garden, and I found myself using any spare minutes in the day to improve the space. I started to learn about plants and flowers and soon discovered which plants are easy to grow and which to avoid. I am still learning but I feel more comfortable now going into a garden centre and asking, "what size pot does this plant need?" and "will this plant grow back next year?" and no one has laughed at me yet.

Finally, going for a local walk was a high point of each day, it reminded me how lucky I am to live in such a beautiful county and why I will never fall out of love with Norfolk.

I believe in the saying knowledge is power. We don't know what the future of this virus holds, but whatever it brings, hopefully we can use what we have learnt from the last year when we react and respond to any challenges that lay ahead.

I hope our current position is one of strength due to a successful vaccine rollout and we start to find our way back to doing the things we enjoy. I will never forget the examples of how communities reached out to each other over the last year and whilst I am excited for everyone reconnecting with family and friends, I hope that we don't forget there are people not in this fortunate position. It would be great if the kindness and reaching out that happened over the last year could continue and become part of everyday life and we take every opportunity we can to make the world a better place to live.

Thursday 27th May 2021: Wendy Gant

Here we are 12 months on from my last reflections on When The World Paused, and what twelve months of so many mixed emotions.

My confusion over announcements such as 'must take things slowly', 'be careful', then 'have a lovely Christmas'.

Frustration because of selfish people who have their own desires and put everything everyone else is trying to do to keep us safe and beat this pandemic in jeopardy.

Sadness for all the people that have lost their lives to this wretched virus, and for their families.

Concern for businesses and all the financial worries they are suffering.

Pride in bucket fulls for all the wonderful people who have worked non-stop for our wellbeing and put us first before themselves.

Heartache for not jumping in the car and seeing our family. Something which I will never take for granted in the future!!

My parents have stayed safe and well and I have been able to see them masked and socially distanced so I am very lucky.

My son and his family, only 40 minutes away, but we couldn't pop to see them. Something we took so much for granted so many moons ago! We both miss them so but as I write we will be seeing them soon to have that most precious hug. My beautiful granddaughter Thea has blossomed and grown up so much and I feel sad that I've missed that time, and all the sleep overs too, like so many other grandparents.

My daughter has been so brave, not only is she coping with lockdown and two small children she also went through a marriage breakdown, divorce, and house move too. The good side of this was we formed a bubble during the second lockdown and for me, especially, the joy was helping with all the school learning for my lovely grandchildren Jess and Ben. I watched them flourish and felt such a close bond to them both but thank God they are only six and nine as the schoolwork was challenging but good fun and interesting. So different from my children's schooldays and I was struggling then!!

My blessing and joy has been spending this quality time with my husband Bas. We have spent days remembering all the good and bad times during our 48 years together. We have looked through old photographs bringing to life many hours of wonderful times spent with our children. We have played cards, done jigsaws, watched films, documentaries, experimented with cooking. Our daily walks have made us appreciate even more the beauty of our wonderful countryside. We have laughed and argued but above all we had the time to realise what a lovely marriage we have and so glad we bumped into each other all those years ago which only seem like yesterday.

My dream is now for us all to remember all these emotions and take forward the good ones and every so often pause your world and look around at all the wonderful things life brings you.

Friday 28th May 2021: Danielle Warman
It's been said millions of times before, but what a year. Who could have known that we would still be in the midst of a pandemic now, over a year later. I'm not sure how long I thought this would go on for, but I guess I'd hoped that once the vaccination was rolling out we would hear less and less about Covid-19. Reading back on my reflections for When The World Paused last year, I was in full-on new mum mode. This time writing, I feel relatively normal with the latest lifting of restrictions (or as normal as we can be).

We have had a good year. I've forced myself to focus on the positives which has been largely easy. My family is healthy. My little boy (no longer a baby!) is happy and healthy and that's all I could hope for.

I went back to work full time in September, and my husband took over looking after Wesley as we did shared parental leave instead of me taking the full nine months. As I was working from home we still managed to spend a lot of time together. And I guess that's what I've taken from all of this – had we not been in this situation we wouldn't have spent all of this great quality time together as a new family.

I've still not really been able to share Wesley with anyone which has probably been the hardest thing since this all started. My parents are really involved in his life as my mum is basically our child minder Monday to Friday (thanks Mum!) but my in-laws have still only met him the once and we're due to see them this summer, all being well. I've still missed coffee dates, baby groups and meeting other new mums, but I'm sitting on the cards I've been dealt and rolling with it.

This virus is still a worry but I'm thankful that we can now start to get him out doing things and we're trying to get him out doing something new every weekend. It's not just for him either –my husband Adrian and I need it too. Some fun and to get us out of the house for reasons other than work.

Despite not really knowing that many people, Wesley's a little charmer and is always happy to babble and grin at masked-up strangers. I wish I had his confidence!

Saturday 29th May 2021: Lucy Lawson
Who would have thought a year ago that we'd still be affected by the pandemic now? A year ago today, on the day of my first reflections for When The World Paused, we were allowed to drive up to five miles from home for the first time in two months. Today, I am grateful for the freedom we now have to travel further: I am writing this from the outer Shetland Island of Papa Stour which has a population of less than 20 people.

I've brought my camper van (a lockdown purchase) with me and over two days I have walked the entire coastline in the best weather we've had so far this year. I have seen the most spectacular scenery and varied wildlife; sea stacks, natural arches, blow holes, Arctic Skuas, and many seals. I spent yesterday evening chatting to friendly and welcoming locals for hours. To me, this is Shetland at its best, and nearly back to normal.

I can't say I've enjoyed lockdowns, restrictions, and cancelled plans but I am grateful to have been in Shetland and to have outdoor space accessible to me. On one hand I feel I've achieved very little in the last year when compared with initial plans, but on the other hand I have managed to swim in the sea every week even through the coldest and wildest months and I'm also grateful for the time that afforded me with a friend when we couldn't meet people inside.

I hated the lack of freedom we've had, but I feel very free now sitting here writing this in my van overlooking the sea, waiting for the ferry home.

Things really are getting better now aren't they...

I've not seen friends and family back in England for over 18 months but I now feel confident enough to have booked flights for September. We'll all have had our second vaccination by then so it should be as safe as it can be.

I'm so grateful for the vaccine roll out. I had my first vaccination four weeks ago and was so impressed with the friendly and efficient delivery by the NHS. I feel very much for those in countries worse off, such as India and Nepal, who are in a critical state with the pandemic. I am attending a yoga fundraiser tomorrow to support them in a small way.

Things that were normal before are now super exciting… in person yoga classes start next week, kayak club has resumed, and a good friend who I've so missed has booked us a day out and afternoon tea for September, I can't wait!

I hugged a friend last weekend; it was lovely and emotional and certainly something I used to take for granted.

I observed with interest how we all found different parts of the pandemic the most difficult, and the reflections in this journal really demonstrate that. The pandemic showed how different we all are, and how wonderful that is, or our lives would be very dull indeed!

Fingers crossed the vaccine rollout continues well and normality keeps on returning… our shrunken worlds are getting bigger again.

Sunday 30th May 2021: Anita Hamer

Am I allowed to start this by saying that I haven't exactly not found these last 14 months or so particularly unpleasant? Let me explain, and I mean what I say from an entirely selfish point of view because it has been the hardest and cruellest of times for so many but when you are a long-term sufferer of anxiety and depression being forcibly told to stay and home and not see anyone, it also feels like a wish that has been granted. However, I am going to be bold and say that was then and this is now; so where do I start some 14 months later?

Myself and my partner moved last year from our little lodge by the water's edge to a house in a nearby town centre and I absolutely love it. It is not a large and busy town by any means but its location means that now, as we are gradually returning to normality, I have to learn to interact with people again from my lovely regular neighbours to the owners of the Italian and the Turkish restaurants that are a few doors up and on the corner by the once again busy market square. Saying good afternoon or good evening to the diners out on the street enjoying their food in the sunshine as I pass by makes me feel part of society and I realise what I have been missing. I feel part of a community which is entirely new to me.

Being able to enjoy my craft as a makeup artist once again from 12th April has also brought me even more joy and contentment than it did before; meeting a bride-to-be who has been able to book her wedding again and start wedding preparations again with confidence is a definite feel-good factor. Families are so grateful and happy to be able to be with one another again and celebrate (albeit in a still limited manner) a joyous occasion. Being around ladies with the biggest smiles on their faces, hearing laughter between friends and families, and feeling genuine palpable love is completely infectious and I leave with a fuzzy feeling every single time.

Feeling brave, I headed off to the cinema today; granted, I booked the earliest time possible to see my film of choice and sat amongst a few like-minded individuals who wanted the cinema experience again but not to sit in a crowded screen room. But, like the promotional advert said, you feel part of a community whilst sat watching a film; all laughing, gasping, sitting entranced by the same thing.

We are sociable beings and lockdowns one, two, and three have brought me back to life, which is terribly ironic, and it has been the biggest gift to me that I could ever ask for; so I have learnt over these months that even in the darkest of days there is still opportunity to grow and actually thrive.

Monday 31st May 2021: Liam Weeks

Tuesday 11th February 2020, a day I'd been looking forward to for months! I woke up early and almost pulled the curtains down as I thrust them open. The bright sunshine filled our apartment opposite Yas Island in Abu Dhabi. I admired the Formula One circuit opposite, along with the huge super yachts that belonged to the UAE's ruling family. Thoughts of the Grand Prix later in the year in November entered my mind and how my dad and his mate Pete had just booked flights to come and experience the festivities were soon dismissed. I had a wedding to get to in Dubai! Not just any wedding – my wedding!! My beautiful bride to be, Claire and our two fabulous boys James and Leon were already waiting for me in Dubai. As I drove an hour along the highway to the next emirate, a journey I had made a thousand times before, my mind was wondering to where we'd be in the next year. Where would we be work wise? Where would we be living? Would we spend the summer split between my hometown of Norwich and Claire's family up in Liverpool?

We opted for a small wedding, without telling our families until afterwards. Just the four of us – Claire, James, Leon, and myself, along with the priest and a witness from the church in Jebel Ali. Claire looked absolutely stunning in a beautiful white dress, with James and Leon beaming with pride in their suits and their brown 'wedding shoes' named because their only previous outing was at my sister Abbie's wedding to Scott the previous summer. Leon had designated himself as official photographer with our Polaroid camera – he was darting around the church to line up his shots, with his older brother 'supervising' the shoot.

My dad and his wife Liz were our last visitors to Abu Dhabi in early March, leaving just two days before the borders closed. We would never have imagined that this was the last time we'd see any of our family for the next 15 months. Usually, we would always have visitors every couple of months from home and try to head back to England at every opportunity. Had we known what was in store, I'm certain that we would have had an extra couple of pints of Guinness with Dad for sure!

Covid was the last thing on our minds. This virus had reached the UAE and there was a handful of cases. Just three weeks later, with only 27 confirmed cases in the country, the UAE government took the decision to move all schools and universities to distance learning. We fully supported the decision taken in our adopted country. 10pm curfews were introduced whilst deep sanitisation of public areas took place. This was followed by a full lockdown in April. We could only leave our home to go grocery shopping, something which we tried to limit to once a week. The supermarkets were like something out of a zombie movie. Everyone was temperature checked on entry, with children and the over 60s prohibited. The wearing of masks was now a legal requirement, as was the wearing of disposable gloves. People were avoiding each other in the aisles as if Covid could leap from one shopping trolley to another.

Our family and friends over in the UK were slowly following us and adjusting to the life that we were now accustomed to over in the UAE; we were surprised by how far behind they were but were so happy when restrictions were finally in place to protect our loved ones.

I'm incredibly lucky to have a career working in a coaching role within a professional football club. Our domestic season was originally suspended in March 2020, with the Arabian Gulf League being cancelled in June as we were unable to complete our fixtures. Normally, we travel to Europe for pre-season in a colder climate, but with the borders closed we were unable to travel and forced to spend pre-season in 40 degrees plus, it was HOT. In a training camp in Al Ain we had positive cases detected within our squad and had to quarantine for two weeks. Being away from the family is always hard but being locked in a 'cell' measuring six metres by six metres is absolute torture. Meals were left outside our doors and we weren't allowed to leave our rooms. We were due to compete in the Asian Champions League in August in Qatar but following a positive case within the squad we were all subjected to another 14-day hotel quarantine in Abu Dhabi and had to withdraw from the tournament. Trying to keep a group of 30 elite athletes physically and mentally fit during this period was very challenging. We used Zoom to hold training sessions. We focused more on the mental side of things than the physical. Keeping our players interacting with each other long after the session had finished. As a group, we have certainly grown a lot closer over the past year, of which we have spent close to four months in hotels away from our families.

The new season got the go ahead in mid-October. Throughout the domestic campaign we have been hit by mini outbreaks within the players and staff, despite our best efforts and constant bloody testing! Testing, testing, and more testing. Since March I have had 129 tests. We get tested three days before every game. Tested after every game. During an outbreak we get tested every day. We get tested to enter the Emirate of Abu Dhabi, as there's now a physical border on entering from Dubai, with a negative PCR test needed from the last 48 hours.

More recently, in April, we competed in the 2021 AFC Champions League. Our group was based in Goa, India, qualifying after we defeated Al Zawraa from Iraq in the play-off. Testing every other day as we battled through six games in 18 days. Our players were exceptional and despite the disadvantage of kicking off less than an hour after breaking the Ramadan fast, we qualified for the last 16 of the tournament. It was the team spirit that had been built up over the past year that got us through. Everyone fighting for his teammate, giving his absolute all for the team, and then going again two days later.

Travelling around Goa, just as India was starting to record world record highs for positive cases, one thing became apparent very quickly, being able to social distance IS a privilege. Everywhere we went there were just people living on top of each other. India came into a national lockdown in the last few days of the tournament. We were helping the hotel staff, and the local support staff to get home to their cities – booking flights and trains for those who had helped us, so that they could get home to their families.

The UAE have led the way with both testing and vaccinations. With such a diverse population the country has been at the forefront of clinical trials with various vaccines from all over the World. We have two vaccines available – Pfizer and Sinopharm, a Chinese vaccine. In Abu Dhabi we had two doses of the Chinese vaccine, with government approval for emergency use being granted in November. I've now had a third booster shot, as a recent immunity test showed that I was below the recommended levels.

The boys have been incredible over the past 14 months. James has been exceptional in his approach to the virtual classroom, taking himself off to his room to crack on with his studies on his iPad. Leon too has really come on recently, thanks in part to his teaching assistant Belinda, who sits with him for hours each day completing his tasks. I can't give the boys enough credit or tell them how proud I am of them and the way that they've dealt with the pressures and frustrations of the pandemic. Whilst being away from their classmates and family, we've made sure that they have had regular catch ups over video calls with Gary and Kathleen in Liverpool and Ange and Ian, Paul, and Liz in Norwich. The boys really look forward to speaking with their grandparents and can't wait to hopefully see them all again soon.

Claire too has been incredible in her resolve during the pandemic. Her new company is really taking off and I'm so incredibly proud of her for the way she manages the family and her business at the same time.

One of the saddest things during this time for us was losing Keith, my stepdad's father and feeling so helpless as we were so far away and not being there for comfort. We have always seen Keith and Pat as wonderful step-grandparents. Massive hugs and a few pints with Ian and Scott in the Beehive to toast Keith will certainly be very high on the list when we finally get home for a visit.

As a family we cannot wait to get back home, to see our loved ones. This is the longest we have been away from our families and cannot wait to see our grandparents, parents, family, and friends – as soon as we are free to travel to the UK, and people can once again visit us without quarantine in London. To have a cup of tea and let's be honest here, more likely a few Jamesons with Nanny Eileen, or a couple of beers and a bottle of red wine with Nanny June and Grandad Ron, or a few pints and a vodka with Gary and Kathleen in Liverpool, or to have a couple of pints and a gin with Mum and Ian, or to have a beer in Dad and Liz's new 'pub' in their garden and to share a prosecco with Maddy having missed her 21st Birthday. We simply cannot wait!

Tuesday 1st June 2021: Georgie Holmes
One year since lockdown…

Hello, I'm Georgie! I work in the Communications team for a housing association in the east of England. My job focuses on internal communications, which has become even more important now than it ever has been before. For most people, adjusting to this new way of life has come with its challenges. And, for our staff, the new normal of working from home or on their own has been tough. However, despite this, we've all pulled together to make sure that our tenants are supported, especially those who are in vulnerable situations.

To reflect on the last 12 months, I wrote this poem. I wanted to capture just how much we've been through within the last year – the good and the bad. And, finally, to say thank you to everyone across the Group who has worked so hard – we've done it together.

It has been one whole year since lockdown began
And now we're onto our third, which wasn't part of the plan
Despite all the challenges we've come up against
And all the moments we've thought 'wow this is intense'
We've managed to come out stronger than ever before
And hopefully the vaccine means we won't have lockdown number four.

Looking back over all that we've done
And remembering that in some parts we did have some fun
We know this journey has not been the easiest ride
And there have definitely been times where we might have cried
But nevertheless, we are so very proud
And we want to say thank you, oh so very loud.

On 23 March we had to adjust to this new way of life
Moving to a digital world which caused quite a strife
We said goodbye to our offices for just a little while
And launched a 'Happy News' to try and make people smile

It's been strange seeing colleagues only via video on Microsoft Teams
And the amount of times we've said 'you're on mute' might make you want to scream.

We always made sure to check if our customers were ok
Many welfare calls were made, sometimes just to say 'hey'
We delivered food parcels to those who couldn't leave their home
And throughout it all, we remained at the end of the phone
Our Kindness fund brought a little joy to some amongst all the sadness
Alongside our charity Hopestead's initiatives, which helped through the madness.

Throughout the pandemic, we've all played our part
Some of us were furloughed and for some it was just the start
Our engineers continued to keep people safe in their home
And our operatives had to somehow adjust to working on their own
We've created makeshift desks, some have used an ironing board we've heard
And for some of us we've become teachers which seems quite absurd.

So, let's say goodbye to the last year and all that we've learned
And look forward to seeing each other in person, for this we have yearned
Let's pat ourselves on the back, it's been quite a run
And look forward to days when we can have fun in the sun
So grateful for everyone's support throughout
We couldn't have done it without each other, of this there is no doubt.

Wednesday 2nd June 2021: Kate Burrows
Lockdown life continued…

Reading back on my reflections in last year's When The World Paused journal, I noted how I focused on the positives, and have I had to do that a lot the last year! I cannot focus on the negative stuff so every week I work out what has been good in the week. Some weeks it was something as simple as being able to go for a walk when it wasn't raining, others like this week is that we can celebrate my dad's birthday this week with a BBQ in the garden like normal. Last year it was his 70th and whilst we could meet in gardens, it was very restricted. So we could not all be together. This year there will be eight of us in the garden to celebrate with him. Still very distanced obviously (goes without saying). So whilst it will still not be the celebration I know he wanted, it will be the first time both my brothers and I will have been in the same garden as my parents for over a year.

My world as I said before shrunk to my home and garden as I work from home and my little bubble is still that. That first lockdown with the sunshine made it all that bit easier. The last lockdowns from October to now I found different and much harder. I had just got used to trying to leave my home and start to cautiously do things and then we were back indoors and had to stay local! Couldn't even go for our winter walks on the beach which I missed more than I thought I would. Whilst I tried to do my daily walk, especially from January onwards, it was harder to find the motivation to do so. I did go but there were days I did not enjoy the walks. Then the snow came and that was good fun (we even built a snowman!) Then back to wet cold days.

If I had written this post last week I think it would have been different as not having any sunshine (it was May, where had the sun gone!) was getting to me, but after three days of glorious sunshine for the bank holiday break I am much more positive.

We felt like we had a little mini break, saw friends, pottered around in the garden... well my husband Simon did lots of work in the garden whilst I supervised from my chair in the garden sunbathing reading a book and eating a lot of crisps! I think I got the better end of that deal.

I feel more positive, than I did a month ago, I am very careful about who I see and what we do. I still have my wobbles, but I am determined to still do things so I do not turn into a hermit. As it would be really easy to not leave the house now after all these lockdowns.

Whilst I miss the ease of life before lockdown, it has helped focus on the important things. Sitting and seeing my friends and family in their gardens or ours has been lovely. There have been many days of lots of layers, jumpers, coats, waterproofs and blankets and we have been very cold whilst sitting in their gardens but just to see them from a distance and not on a video call was one of the nicest things from easing out of lockdown.

So was walking by the sea again. To hear the waves crashing about after what felt like years (only months of course) was soothing. Whilst there was no going to a café for breakfast instead we just took our own picnic, but enjoying being out and about for one of the first times this year.

Thursday 3rd June 2021: Candice Liverpool
June 2021

The month we have all been waiting for! Who would have thought that one year, two months, and eleven days on we would still be living with restrictions? But there IS light at the end of the tunnel…

So much has changed for me personally since March 2020. I was a police officer back then. Skip forward to April 2021 and I retired, through ill health, and am left feeling like the world, my world, is unrecognisable.

Dealing with PTSD and anxiety during a global pandemic is no mean feat! Prior to 2020 my lovely doctor 'prescribed' me time with friends, once a week. Time to spend away from my partner and daughter (they were at the incident that caused my PTSD so I needed to have some detachment) having a coffee, going for a walk, or watching a film. Although some weeks it was hard to get out, I always felt much better after seeing a good friend; chatting, laughing, and putting the world to rights. Then Boris announced that we couldn't see anyone, and had to stay at home, and my whole world collapsed. While others seemed to be lapping up the time at home, enjoying the lockdown sunshine and the slower pace of life, I felt like I was trapped with my trauma and thoughts, and my anxiety just got worse.

2020 was tough for me. Of course I managed to paint that smile on and hide the true effect that lockdown – coupled with my trauma – was having on me but it was tough.

Then it happened, the realisation that my favourite time of year, Christmas, was cancelled and that just broke me.

I have always been a positive person, my glass wasn't just half full but wildly overflowing, however, I was really struggling to find the positives in a world that appeared broken.

In February I had a birthday. Looking back to the previous year's celebrations I felt a pang of disappointment and sadness that this one wouldn't be quite the same. I was one of the lucky ones that got to celebrate in 2020 with no restrictions and (I thought) this year was going to be rubbish in comparison. But, I can officially say my lockdown birthday was one of the best I ever had…

I had visits from people that I wouldn't have normally seen (because people made an extra effort).

My darling daughter Bella and partner Paul threw me a lovely at home party (no need to pay for taxis).

I drank Prosecco and gin all day!! (No different to any other birthday to be honest).

I ate food all day and didn't have to worry about fitting into a nice outfit as I wasn't going anywhere (loungewear is the future).

Most importantly, I remembered that birthdays are about who you get to spend them with, not grand gestures or expensive presents (although Paul if you're reading this, they do help!)

This was a turning point for me and there was a shift in my mindset. The world had changed, my life had changed, and yes, the bad days still happen. PTSD is with me every day and I'm still learning to respect it and how it impacts me. But my life isn't over and as that light at the end of the tunnel brightens, I am loving being able to see my friends' faces, give hugs, go on date nights, visit my parents and sister, watch Bella play with her friends, and make plans for the future.

I owe so much to my family and friends that have supported

me. Who have had their own stuff going on but still reached out and said: "You got this".

And now?

I am just excited to get back on track with my doctor's advice and start planning those coffee and cakes dates – how amazing are our NHS?

Friday 4th June 2021: Robert Gant

Firstly, my heart goes out to all of the people and families that have been gravely affected by Covid.

It has been over a year now since the pandemic began and I got used to a new way of 'lockdown living'. Covid, for me, has taken away a lot of the spontaneity of the everyday and made me understand how I took things for granted.

I've missed all of my family immensely.

Mum, Dad, Sara, Jess, Ben, Grandma, Grandad, and Great Aunt Joyce – not being able to physically be there all of the time has been so tough. Love you all lots.

We were now living in RobertMichelleTheatropolis – that is myself, my wife, and my daughter were a lockdown household. My parents, sister, niece and nephew, grandparents, great aunt, aunties, uncles, cousins, and in-laws were now outside of this.

Thank goodness for technology! FaceTime, video calls, Zoom meetings were the new forms of visual communication and allowed me to keep in touch. I remember my first video call to my parents after the first lockdown was announced and how it felt comforting but also strange to think that this was going to be the new visual communication with them – and for how long?

Being in lockdown brought many changes to family life. Gone was a lot of the everyday routine and we now had to adapt to a new way of living. We would go out for walks, if permitted, and Michelle would go shopping for groceries once a week.

What was Covid? We had to stop socialising with others outside and sanitise/wash our hands after being outside. In RobertMichelleTheatropolis we would do what we could from sanitising the groceries with anti-bac wipes before putting them away, to sanitising the post that came through the letterbox, to wiping down door handles, amongst other measures. As an individual, I had my indoor and outdoor clothes routine, especially as the pandemic lengthened and lockdown changes allowed us to go out more. Until now I still do this and I think probably until my second jab I will be operating my clothes policy: indoor clothes for inside and outside clothes for outside until washed and then I could choose again!

Running her business from home, adapting, spending more time together, trying to find things we both liked to watch on TV, being a brilliant mum, being the cornerstone of the household, and even running this When The World Paused journal and publishing a book for NHS charities – my wonderful wife Michelle. Love you darling.

"Dad, I'm bored and miss my friends", "Dad, you are not as good as my teachers at school", "Dad, can I have a break now?", "Dad, can we go on the trampoline?" and *"Dad I think you are a good teacher really".*

These were the words of my beautiful daughter Thea. Love you sweetheart.

Home schooling brought a variety of emotions, from seeing how much my daughter missed her school, school friends, and teachers to being able to teach and watch my daughter learn whilst not being at school. I now have a greater admiration than I already had before for all schoolteachers and school staff for the wonderful job that they do teaching our children and building their future. As a home schooler for about three months I would like to say to all teachers and teaching staff, in my daughter's words: good job!

NHS and key workers: you are all fantastic, even before the pandemic, but how you put others before yourselves is nothing short of honourable. In RobertMichelleTheatropolis we clapped/banged pans for you all as a household every week.

Thank you.

I have always found understanding how our world works and the science behind it fascinating. I would like to thank all of the brilliant scientists and people involved in producing Covid vaccinations for their hard work and dedication in this momentous achievement.

The first hugs with my parents, sister, niece, and nephew a couple of weeks ago was lovely and it is starting to feel as if things are getting back to how they were before Covid, slowly but surely. We have started doing things again – going out for something to eat and drink, my daughter is playing tennis, going to gymnastics, and karate. It's not quite the same with the masks/hand gel but things are getting there.

I wish everyone all the best for the future as the world begins to un-pause.

Saturday 5th June 2021: Haze Carver
Menopause and Malbec

Text message sent to work, March 20th, 2020:
Hi, it's looking like today will more than likely now be Harriet's last day of primary school and Sully's for Reception (sad emoji face). I have to bring home their past work and collect their future work/learning – I'll finish at 2.30 today to collect them if that's ok? (crying emoji)

That text was sent three hundred years ago, but it was only last year.

What I remember of February 2020 was a month of school gate gossiping, WhatsApp speculations and shouting up the stairs, "…it's on telly again and it's getting really bad in Italy!"

No-one seemed to have any answers and all I had was questions.

Why was all the pasta being bought, but not the pesto? What's wrong with pesto? What are you meant to stock up on when you know carbs go straight to your menopausal middle? Do you think this is what Mum had at Christmas? Why loo roll? Does Covid give you diarrhoea? Why has a 20kg bag of potatoes turned up when I only ordered 2kg?

I got really nervous when I couldn't buy Calpol. That to me was apocalypse fodder. I'm sure we all have a zombie apocalypse plan, and raiding the little pharmacy was top of my list after covering my body in magazines and electrical tape.

After that Monday night announcement of the first lockdown by the prime minister, I spent all night thinking (or trying not to think) 'how will we cope with it all?'

My partner and I both work full time, we have a 10-year-old, and a five-year-old who now needed to be home-schooled. We were absolutely sure of two things: between us we had no experience of teaching and zero patience.

We weren't alone in that, and despite the difficult times in lockdown I am thankful that we were lucky in so many ways with our situation, and that is something I'll carry with me forever.

Friends
I was really ill that first week of lockdown – I'd wake up in the night feeling like I couldn't breathe, I didn't have the cough, but I couldn't taste anything. I don't know if I had it, but just as I started to feel better, the heating packed in. We couldn't have the heating people in because we were self-isolating. It got so cold, and I didn't want the kids getting ill, so popped a message on Facebook and within a couple of days we were all snug in the lounge with five cosy oil radiators. It felt like an adventure to the kids to wear three jumpers and drink hot chocolate for those two weeks.

With the absence of after school clubs, grandparents, work commutes we found we had time. Not a lot, as juggling a working day, teaching two kids, cooking, cleaning and most importantly ensuring the children feeling safe and secure (mainly consisting of fruit smoothies and telly) was really hard. But we did get to sit together and eat dinner together. It was lovely! We had Spanish nights, Japanese nights…we took turns cooking and played silly games – such a simple pleasure, but one we'd been missing!

With only one hour to get out in the day, we loved exploring our neighbourhood – we found lovely woods nearby and just enjoyed the screen-free time together. We painted eggs and hung them in the woods for Easter and when we passed other people out walking, they smiled. I've always been a 'Hello'er so it felt good that even though the streets were quiet, you were greeted with 'we know how you're feeling' smiles. As the nights were so light, we started up 'family fun' after dinner. We took over our quiet cul-de-sac and had football matches together, badminton games, and we chalked on every inch of the road. We designed robots, under-sea homes, spaceships, and left messages for our neighbours.

Decluttering
Spending so much time at home really awoke the minimalist in me. We're not hoarders, but we definitely had so much 'stuff'. It's the things that you accumulate without replacing: bed linen, cookware, plates etc (thirty mugs? Really?). Working from home made me realise we had things we just didn't use. It started slowly, but I gradually went through the whole house, and as it started to empty, I felt free and light. Tidying became a doddle because what we did have, had a home. It's an ongoing journey for me, but lockdown gave me the time to see how it improved our lives. I find visual clutter so distracting. Two skips later and I'm happy (yes, you can manage with just two saucepans!)

What makes me smile these days, is that I used to dread wet summer holidays – what would we do all day with the kids? I worried about finding things to do for a few days if we were stuck inside. We were stuck in for weeks and weeks, and you know what? It was actually ok. We had fun. We're a good team, a great team.

So many businesses talk about how they pivoted to stay afloat throughout the pandemic, families had to do that too. Crazy working hours, endless snacking requests, back-bedroom offices with mid-week glasses of red in the back garden. If you home schooled you deserve a lifetime of back rubs and spa weekends.

My biggest thank you (after the NHS) is to all the other parents who shared their struggles and tears, it felt good to know you were not alone.

So, here's to old friends that stayed with us throughout lockdown ... Menopause and Malbec. It doesn't look like they're going anywhere.

Sunday 6th June 2021: Gemma Brown

When thinking about these reflections, I really stumbled over trying to capture the enormity of this year. I was struck by the feeling that so much has happened in one year, but also so little. Is it really possible that what has happened has really happened?! The words I've written fail to do it justice – the change, the growth, the loss, but also the hope.

There aren't that many times when I reflect back on a period of 12 months. Save perhaps for 1st January or significant birthdays. This feels significant because of the global impact we all have felt. Whatever circumstances or personal experience, the pandemic has affected all of us at the same time. And that is a lot to get my head around.

If I could go back to this time last year, I would say to myself: "You will be ok."

12 months ago I was riding the coronacoaster; feeling a lot of anxiety and overwhelm that I really hadn't experienced before. I was worried on a daily basis, I was exhausted, I consumed too much news. There was a lot of fear but also, great things have happened too.

I've taken the time and opportunity for internal reflection and along the journey have come to know myself better. At times that's been wonderfully freeing and at others completely draining as the cogs turn at a relentless pace. In taking time for me, and questioning who I am and what I want in the face of a pandemic, I've come to value simplicity. The simple things really are the big things. I knew that before, but I have come to truly feel it.

Morning walks
Taking time to be grateful. A walk taken in my village a thousand times, but always seeing something new. The closeness of family and friends and important conversations. A

time for quiet and stillness. The beauty of nature. The ability to prioritise my self-care.

This time has reassuringly reminded me of what is important to me and how much I am nurtured by the simple things. Not only have I been reminded, but I feel freer to 'own' them – where before I may have hid them in the background. My love for being at home, for spending time alone, for quiet and calm, seeing seedlings grow day by day, for a morning walk with my dog, for not overcommitting, for deep conversation, for an early night… These never seemed that 'fun' or exciting. But now I know they are fun and exciting for me.

With joy in the simple things, I have also stepped out of my comfort zone on numerous occasions. I've been bold to try things that scared me previously, I've given things a go – worrying less about it going 'wrong' or looking 'bad'. Small things like taking up cycling, saying no, and networking online, or bigger things like presenting to 200 people for the first time on a Zoom workshop. With so much tragedy and pain going on around the world, I saw these new things and thought 'what's the worst that can happen, have a go'. So I did.

Now as we start to emerge out of lockdown, I fully hope to retain my new relationships with simplicity and courage and carry forth to welcome whatever lies ahead.

Monday 7th June 2021: Eddie West-Burnham
Well, wasn't that a fun year!

I didn't realise this till quite recently, but the expression: 'May you live in interesting times' isn't as straightforward as it seems. On the face of it, it feels like a blessing, however the expression is normally used ironically; life is actually much better in 'uninteresting times' of peace and tranquillity than in 'interesting' ones, which are usually times of trouble. Ain't that the truth! Added to that, although it is well known as an English expression, it is actually a translation of a traditional Chinese curse…

What wouldn't we give to be back in our 'uninteresting times' of pre-Covid – relative peace and tranquillity, accepting that even then it was pretty challenging for many of us. Having been made redundant in Sept 2019, I launched into the world of self-employment last February as I started my new career as a freelance coach and consultant – arguably not the best timing! Things started well, I had some really interesting charity consultancy work and a couple of great coaching clients. Then on 16th March we were told to limit non-essential contact with others, stop all unnecessary travel, work from home and 'avoid pubs, clubs, theatres and other such social venues…'

A week later the shutters came down on the country and my new career. The first lockdown got underway, as did my relatively short career as a home schooler to my two daughters. For many of us it was the start of a year like no other.

Unless directly affected it's hard for many of us to comprehend the devastating impact that Covid has had for many families – to put it in context, it was the underlying cause of more deaths in 2020 than any other infectious diseases since 1918. Leaving the politics aside, the pandemic has brought a new awareness of existing problems that need addressing with some urgency; the growing challenges of mental ill health, health inequalities, and domestic violence, have all worsened during the pandemic.

The economic impact has been massive for millions of people. The furlough scheme, which has provided essential financial help for struggling businesses, has been a life saver for many people, even if many thousands of us didn't qualify because we hadn't been self-employed long enough – I guess you win some, you lose some!

Now that all sounds pretty negative, but on reflection I have had a pretty good year. While I was shocked at how difficult it has been coming to terms with being made redundant, I now have a degree of insight and empathy which I could never have hoped to acquire if I hadn't had this time.

The real bonus has been the time I spent with my daughters. At times I found home schooling really hard, not just that maths is done so differently to when I left school 40 years ago, but like many others, I found it impossible to effectively home school and set up a new business at the same time; in trying to do both I risked failing at both. It was an easy decision; the girls would have my (almost) undivided attention. That said, we could only do this effectively because my wonderful wife works as a senior NHS manager and we had the technology to make it work – putting us in a better position than many. Added to this, I volunteered for the NHS which meant the girls could go to school a couple of times a week giving us all a break!

We cooked.
We made things.
We made the best of it.

Without lockdown, would I have had the chance to spend so much time with my girls as I did over the last year? Not a chance. This was a precious time, stolen time, that I will never get again.

All that AND, just three days before the first lockdown, Reggie the hound joined the family!

What did I miss over the lockdown? Yomping around Sandringham and walking on the beach and stopping for a donut, going on holiday, heading out for a curry and a pint, going to the cinema. I really missed seeing my son and his family and my brothers.

I also really missed having a job. Having a job gives us structure, purpose and meaning, it is a massive part of our identity, helping shape who we are – without it we're at risk of being rudderless. Being made redundant hit me harder that I thought it would. That said, I love my new career as a coach and all the opportunities it gives me to serve and support people in new and interesting ways.

As a family we have been incredibly fortunate. We avoided many of the devastating impacts that Covid unleashed upon society. The fragility of life has been rudely exposed without any element spared; family life, where and how we work, increased levels of loneliness, our health (especially mental health) and relationships have been put to the test. Paradoxically, I'd like to think that the restrictions that have kept us apart and stopped us from going to work, school, the gym, the pub, and so on have actually brought us closer together as a family.

Throughout all this, my Mrs. W-B has been awesome – my love, my life, my beautiful wife.

So, what next? Well, later this month I start a part time coaching contract which will be the platform to relaunch my career as coach, mentor, and consultant.

As the world of work opens up again, and we start to realign to the new normal, we all could use a little assistance getting back to our best. Use whatever works best for you, I'd suggest a coach is the perfect partner to help navigate through the obstacles and challenges places and get back on top of things. I've no doubt it will take a while to assess the long-term impact of the pandemic, but I would like to believe that we'll learn from it and become better human beings as a result of it.

Tuesday 8th June 2021: Suzanna Wood

It didn't hit me as to how serious Covid would be until the announcement came that schools would be closing. I worried about how to tell my daughters, Emily aged 9 and Bethany aged 6 at the time. Many children in their school had already stopped attending and as parents at the school gate, there was lots of speculation.

I will never forget their last day at school, they came out beaming with their arms full of Mother's Day cards and presents (donated by their school PFA which was lovely) along with exercise books, home learning and reading books. I had offered to collect some schoolwork for a family whose children were already isolating and I remember leaving their house in tears as it hit me that we didn't know when we would see them again and when my girls would go back to school.

Watching the news that weekend made the future feel bleak and there was no sense of when it would be over and how bad it would get.

The school had given my girls a diary to record their thoughts and feelings during lockdown. My 6-year old's first entry was: "Covid is scary, I don't want my grandad to die." It was heartbreaking to read and we had lots of tears that evening. He wasn't ill, it was just her first thought after hearing the media speculation on television.

Times were tough for her; she had an amazing sleepover planned with her friends in early April for her birthday and it had to be cancelled. She did get a sleepover with her sister though and those of her friends who lived close by made her cards and visited her on the doorstep as part of their daily exercise, it brought a smile to her face.

I also started a new role that month, trying to get up to speed with what was expected alongside teaching two children was tough. The school were sending us work that was fun and it made it much easier to get the children to engage. We made a bug hotel one day and got awarded the green Blue Peter badge from the children's television show for it a few months later.

In those summer months, I spent time getting to know my children and my husband again. We slowed down without the commute to the office and the constant juggle with childcare to ensure that we could both work full-time. Luckily, our family lived close by to help us and we couldn't have done it without them! We spent our lockdown evenings in the garden, had movie nights, we sang and danced, did pottery painting and jewellery making and we laughed so much.

We also spent lots of time walking, rediscovering our village and I focused on my running, building up to the Great North Run and the virtual London Marathon. My biggest achievements to date!

As the restrictions were relaxed, we had a perfect two weeks off in August where we felt quite free, holidaying in Dorset with masks and hand sanitiser, which by then felt quite normal. We played on the beach, ate fish and chips, and had many evenings of Cluedo, our favourite game. We questioned if this life was the new normal?

The girls went back to school in September and they were so excited, they accepted their teachers in face masks and hand sanitiser in their pencil cases as it didn't matter; they were back with their friends. They relished the chance to learn again in a classroom.

As the evenings started getting darker and winter was coming, I made sure I ran in daylight hours to get me through. I love the sunshine and the summer months so I knew it would be a struggle. It wasn't as bad as I thought though. I had the time to focus on my job with the children being back at school and the days flew by.

Christmas came quickly and always a big celebration in my house, we had plans with family which had to be cancelled at the last minute due to the next lockdown but we still had fun, spending parts of the day on Zoom to ensure that no one felt left out. I selfishly enjoyed the time as just the four of us again.

So we found ourselves back to home schooling in January and schools had much higher expectations this time around! There were online classes to attend, Maths and English that had to be completed along with a full-time job to do. I'm so lucky that I work for an organisation who put their staff and their families first as I could never have got through this winter lockdown. It was cold, dark, and gloomy! We were encouraged to get out during the day for a walk in the daylight and to take breaks from the screen. This was much needed and kept me sane.

Moving to the here and now, I've just had a week off work as its half term. We had days out, the girls went to sleepovers at their friends' houses and we went to Wales for the weekend to visit my brother and his fiancé. Our first trip there as they moved just before lockdown. The sun shone and it felt like normal life was on its way.

I think back to the last year with positive thoughts, I would never have got that time to spend with my husband and daughters, renewing our family bond and enjoying a much slower pace of life. I even ran a marathon which I never thought possible! I asked my eldest daughter to sum up her favourite part of lockdown and she said home school and spending time together. I must have done something right.

My last thoughts are with those who were in the frontline during the pandemic, I know their experiences will be nothing like mine, they couldn't stay home and enjoy life in the slow lane with their families. I want to thank them for all they did to keep us safe.

Wednesday 9th June 2021: Edward Murray aged 13
Good Things
Looking back on the last year I realise that it's been mostly good. For me, the good things have included spending (even) more time outside, having time with my family, not working to a strict school timetable and routine, and having the opportunity to do things that I wouldn't normally have time for. Things like gardening (I am a top carrot grower!), helping my dad build a shed, playing tennis with my mum. I realised how much I enjoy certain school subjects and was able to spend more time on them, particularly geography, history and perfecting my fish sketching and drawing skills!

The Not So Good Things
The last year has had its ups and downs. I missed seeing my friends and wider family, at times I felt lonely and in need of a change of company. During the dark, wet winter months I started to feel claustrophobic and cage mad! My world shrank and during the worst of the weather it was really hard to get out for runs or a cycle ride, I really didn't enjoy those few weeks. I felt like I was working all the time, stuck staring at a screen, it was hard to stay motivated.

The Easing of Lockdown
When the Government announced that lockdown was easing, I was pleased but also nervous. Would I be able to keep up at swimming or know how to play football? Would it all come back, or would I have lost my skills and fitness? Would school make us do lots of extra catch-up work and how would school and my friends have changed?

What I have learnt
These are some of the things that I have learnt about myself and people in the last year.

I am more resilient – I can get through difficult things.

I am not alone, lots of people felt similar things to me.

I feel stronger for trying new things and pushing myself to do them.

I realised how much I like going to school and that my school is the right one for me.

I listened to the news a lot over the last year and heard a lot about inequalities, like racism, and food poverty. Footballer Marcus Rashford's campaign made me aware of food poverty and unequal opportunities in this country. I wasn't as aware of these issues before Covid.

My hopes for the future
I hope that Covid will pass, that everyone will be vaccinated. I hope the Government will pay more interest to children's wellbeing, food poverty, and climate change.

Thursday 10th June 2021: Vicki Haverson

When we first went into lockdown in March 2020 it gave me the opportunity to slow down from a hectic pace of travel and spend time in the new surroundings I'd recently moved to with my husband and two dogs.

Over time, and as the pandemic continued, the work I do in leadership development had me thinking a lot about our uniqueness as individuals, the strengths we contribute, the needs we have and what triggers us to behave the way we do.

There has been a lot of focus on the expectations of leaders and how these might have changed as a result of the pandemic. It turns out we have the same expectations now as we've always had, it's that the crisis has revealed where they aren't being met.

During last year I spent a lot of time reflecting on my personal values, my strengths, and their needs. It led me to challenging and reconfirming what my own non-negotiables are and I took the decision to leave my job back in August.

Our emotional health can be disrupted by the things that happen, leading to feelings of anxiety, fear, stress, sadness and overwhelm, and on the flipside happiness, relief, and excitement. I felt all of these emotions after making such a big decision, sometimes within the same hour.

I didn't quite have my 'what next' figured out and took on one of Michelle's (Gant) important mottos: focus on what you can control and influence – and let the rest be.

It was during this time I realised how important my network and friends were as well as staying true to my values and my strengths in looking at opportunities for the future. I also had an increasing feeling of wanting to give something back and serve a greater purpose.

In November I began working part-time for Greenacre Group to help support them in growing their consulting business, Greenacre Consult. There is a real alignment with my values and my strengths and I love every minute of the work I'm doing which is helping organisations in the housing sector grow and develop their leadership talent and realise the potential of their people.

Before lockdowns I knew managing my energy rather than time was important, yet it wasn't something I'd ever been able to truly get to grips with. Managing my personal energy is now something I do deliberately and consciously because I know results reflect behaviours and these are driven by my physiological state. I try hard to make sure I get enough sleep, eat well, walk in nature, and build in transitions throughout the day rather than always moving onto the next thing straightaway. Whilst it's always not perfect, what I do know is that when I do follow this through I not only feel better, I get better results.

When I look back over the last year at a time when we have been largely confined to our homes because of the pandemic, the wheels of life have kept turning and things have still happened. Like:

- The flood water that engulfed the entire downstairs of our new home in the early hours of Christmas Eve morning.
- The unexpected restrictions at Christmas that stopped us from being able to get together as a family after all the planning and excitement.
- My grandfather turning 90 and only being able to wish him a Happy Birthday through a window. And not being able to visit him in hospital where he spent a month after a fall.
- Leaving a job and getting a new one.
- The loss of my mother-in-law.

- My sister getting pregnant with her first child and moving a 10-minute drive away after years of living thousands of miles from each other
- Getting on a train again for the first time in over 12 months to meet my new work colleagues in person.
- Not being able to see my mum and then seeing her again for the first time in seven months.

I remember standing in the kitchen in my wellies white knuckling the worktop to try and steady and calm myself down after realising we'd been flooded on Christmas Eve morning. My husband was outside trying to stop more water coming in and I didn't know where to start with the inside. All that kept going through my mind on repeat was 'why us, why has this happened to us, why on Christmas Eve, why, why, why!' In that moment I was reminded of a Ted Talk I had seen by Lucy Hone where she talks about her own tragedy and some of the tactics she used to get through it. I replaced my 'why me' with 'why not me?' And then asked myself whether what I was doing was helping or harming me.

Thinking this way isn't always easy and it doesn't remove all the negative emotions in a situation. What I have learnt is one of the glorious things about being alive is that there will be moments when something happens that we weren't expecting and didn't want to happen. And when it does it can be helpful to lean into some tools and strategies that can help us.

Friday 11th June 2021: Janet Traynor
'Listen to the Music…'(1)

When I was a child, I, like many would often wish that our school would somehow disappear so you didn't have to do that dreaded test or exam…roll on 44 years later, now I'm an adult who was elated that I didn't have to make that overall one hour journey to work every day. I reckon I have been given nine days of my life back from just travelling and the quality of life generally has been immense; too big to quantify. However, it has come as a huge cost to others – death, Long Covid, or a long-term disability; or wiping out 800,000 years of life in the UK alone(2). Like the major events of the UK's past, this will be remembered for years to come.

One thing that has always been constant this whole time is music, I managed to find songs I hadn't heard for years and all the memories that came rushing back were sometimes quite emotive as it took me back to a place, a time in my life with dear family and friends; quite nostalgic – the words quite meaningful, which I didn't quite appreciate first time round. '…making me feel I'm on top of the world..' '…looking at the world in an optimistic light'(3). 'Miss you'(4) all.

Over the last 15 months we have lived with a pandemic, something our grandparents, never mind our parents had to endure. However, we were never 'Waiting on a War'(5) to start and entertaining Uncle Sam's 'American Patrol…'(6), those 'Boogie Woogie Bugle Boys'(7) our allies. They endured hard times in a different way but VE day brought 'Good Times'(8) ahead. We are close, not long now; just need to keep doing what we are doing right.

The hot 'summer nights'(9) of 2020 were amazing, with 'Perfect Day…'s(10) – taking our breaks from our makeshift home workstations with a walk, sitting in our gardens/outside spaces when normally we were working though our lunches, wishing our lives away for the weekend so we could be in the sun – for just one 'Lovely Day'(11) or a 'Sunny Afternoon'(12), only to find it's raining cats and dogs (not men(13), or women).

People's mental health and wellbeing has suffered greatly generally. In the early days when some of my colleagues who live on their own or had faced some of life's challenges were struggling, we used Microsoft Teams for catch ups and where work nights out were non-existent we didn't let it stop us getting together, albeit virtually, for drinks after work or a music quiz. This did 'Make me Smile' (14).

The autumn and winter months did 'Rock the Boat'(15) of even the most upbeat amongst us, we had been spoilt with the 'Glorious'(16) summer, but, we have lived to tell the tale and hopefully it will be the last of the unfavourable but necessary lockdowns; then we can have the proper family time we have all craved and took for granted pre-Covid. There'll be some levelling up in our own personal lives as we have taken stock of what really matters in that we work to live, not live to work.

'Music is a world within itself with a language we all understand…'(17) this became abundantly clear when I watched a video of 250 musicians in the Netherlands singing their heart out to the Neil Young Rockin' in the Free World(18) – quite moving; a reminder we are still in a free world, Covid won't beat us in the fullness of time, whenever that might be – 'We have all the time in the world…' '…we need nothing more…'(19)

1)Listen to the Music – The Doobie Brothers, 2) Scientific Reports 18/02/21 via The Telegraph, 3) Sunshine – Gabrielle, 4)Miss you – Rolling Stones, 5) Waiting on a War – The Foo Fighters, 6) American Patrol – Glen Miller, 7) Boogie Woogie Bugle Boys – The Andrew Sisters, 8) Good Times – Chic, 9) Summer Nights – John Travolta & Olivia Newton-John, 10) Perfect Day – Lou Reed, 11) Lovely Day – Bill Withers, 12) Sunny Afternoon – The Kinks, 13) It's Raining Men

– The Weather Girls, 14) Make Me Smile – Steve Harley, 15) Rock the Boat – Hues Corporation 16) Glorious – Andreas Johnson, 17) Sir Duke – Stevie Wonder, 18) Rockin' in the Free World – Neil Young, 19) We Have All the Time in the World – Louis Armstrong

Saturday 12th June 2021: Emma Outten

Today I will be crossing the border from Norfolk to Suffolk again, something I have done countless times since my parents' house went up for sale, soon after the easing of restrictions on April 12.

It has been the family home for a good 40 years. Every time I go back there, I plan to clear a room – or at least a cupboard. And each time I get floored by something my mum (a seamstress during the 'golden age' of couture in the '50s) had started making but hadn't finished: from bunting with the pins still in, to a cuddly toy without a face…I can't bear to throw any of it away – not yet, at least.

Like many others, in 2020 I learnt more about loss than ever before. I'd already lost my dad a couple of years earlier, to cancer.

A week into the first lockdown, one of our pet rabbits keeled over and then died in my arms on the way to the vets. A couple of weeks later, we were back at the vets, with his brother. Because of Covid restrictions, I had to wait in the car while they put him to sleep. They'd both lived a long life, for rabbits, but it was still hard to let them go. We buried them both in our garden and I cleared out their hutch one last time.

When restrictions started easing, in May 2020, we were able to visit my mum. The first thing we did was go to the seaside and get her fish and chips. We sat under a gazebo and ate ours while she sat indoors and ate hers. We noticed she didn't finish. In June, when we were able to sit inside and eat with her, in her support bubble, she was still struggling to finish. In July she went to the doctors about her symptoms. In August she was diagnosed with ovarian cancer. In September I took her to an appointment to see the consultant – he took one look at her and went off to see if there was a bed available. In October I watched her take her last breath. The kindly nurse standing by the other side of her bed almost guided me through what to do and say. "She can still hear you", I remember her saying.

I'll never forget how kind the doctors and nurses were that day. NHS workers are heroes every year – not just last year or this year.

I'm aware these aren't the most uplifting reflections. But at least I was one of the lucky ones. I was able to be present when my mum passed away. Her funeral took place during the second lockdown, so there were 30 of us present.

What positives can I take away from the past few months? For one thing, I've learnt about friendships – mine and my mum's. Her neighbours have seen me come and go in the cul-de-sac on a regular basis. There's the neighbour who ferries a lot of my mum's stuff to the local charity shop, where she volunteers – and the one who has taken stuff to the recycling centre. There's the neighbour who came over with tea and cake, the one who came over with wine and cake, and the one who comes over with lunch on a tray. There's the neighbour who chose a favourite garden ornament and made a donation to a cancer charity – and the one who took the afternoon off work, brought his van home, loaded it up, followed me back home and unloaded it all at the other end. Where would we all have been without good neighbours this past year or so?

As for my friends, they know who they are. All have gone the extra mile to help me in my quest not to throw anything into a skip. Some have even stayed with me overnight in the half-empty house. I feel lucky to have such fantastic friends. Friends who know it will be their turn one day.

Then there's my teenage daughter. She may shake her head when I bring back yet another carload of stuff but then she'll get stuck in and find room for it all. She knows she's got a hoarder for a mum and works with it.

My parents were born before the Second World War and before the phrase 'throwaway society' was even a thing. There's 80-odd years of memories to process, and it's all part of my grieving process.

So today I am heading back there. As is my brother, who has the task of going through childhood things in his old bedroom.

I'm not looking forward to having to say a final goodbye to the house and garden my mum loved spending time in. In my small garden I have rehomed a few of her plant pots and I look forward to seeing her flowers bloom each year. What have I learnt about love and loss? Real love never dies. If anything, it just keeps growing.

Sunday 13th June 2021: Tom Holt
Fear of the backslide

It felt like an age, but as a family we have finally been able to let out that long awaited sigh of relief, the people I care most about have all been vaccinated. So why am I more anxious and worried now than I have been at any point throughout the last year?

It turns out that I cope well in an apocalypse, years of living alone prepared me perfectly for those weeks and months of isolation. I found a method that helped me keep it together, it's becoming a bit of a cliché, but how many times in our lives will we ever have the opportunity to stop the planet spinning and really think about where we are at and what we are doing with our lives?

When I asked myself that question I didn't like the answer. I'd spent a decade self-sabotaging and putting all my eggs in the wrong basket. It was well past time for a change, it was time to stop pretending that I was fine and actually do something about it. So, I started to run.

On 28 March 2020 I ran 1.29km at 5m:24s/KM, not very far and not very fast, but it was a start. Somewhere in the back of my mind was the possibility of running the Manchester 10km in May 2020 (please forgive my lockdown naivety). That short run hurt, but after recovering I had a feeling of accomplishment that I'd not felt for a long time. I felt good about myself, at that a time an unnervingly rare phenomenon.

With nothing else to distract me I was able to stick at it. The desire to improve gave me something to focus my attention on during the toughest moments of being totally alone. Slowly but surely I got better, to the point that just over a year later I finished 10th in a 10km race.

My running has given me back a feeling of self-worth that I haven't felt for years, it's been liberating. I follow my Strava stats and times with obsessive regularity, if anyone goes ahead of me on a segment I'm out there the next day trying to get it back.

But this new-found fitness obsession does have a darker side, now there is a creeping anxiety and fear that it's all going to go away. As we start to slowly to see the old world returning I have to face real temptation for the first time. I don't want to go back to the person that I was before March 2020, I need to keep running for my own wellbeing, but the risk of backsliding is always there every time I go for a beer or take a rest day. At its worst, not running can cause full panic, anxiety and curling up in a ball in my living room meltdown. I've never been great at talking about my problems, but opening up to friends and family about those tough moments is real progress for me.

The truth is that in general I'm happier and healthier than I have been for a long time, but that nagging worry is there all the time. If I make a mess of this now, there won't be another pandemic on hand to rescue me. So, I've taken some steps to try mitigating that potential disaster.

In another lockdown cliché, I've got myself a puppy (Henry, a now 8-month-old black Labrador) who has given me a responsibility to always be up and moving even when I don't feel like it, that helps. I've also already registered for the rescheduled Manchester 10k in September and will be raising money for Cancer Research UK to give me that extra motivation to continue to commit to my training.

Being open is not a personality trait I am particularly blessed with, writing so honestly is something that I wouldn't have been capable of a year ago. If running has given me back my self-worth, then being willing to accept my weaknesses is a symptom of that. I fear the old me, I don't want that person to come back and sabotage me again. Here's hoping the pandemic has changed my life permanently for the better.

Monday 14th June 2021: Eliza Warden
After Plague

The pandemic settled into my life in the same way one might settle into their favourite armchair, or against an old pillow. It was familiar to not speak to anyone for days, to not leave the house, to avoid touch as if I were a leper, for the good of others. This time, it wasn't self-imposed. This time, it was by necessity, and at the same time as everyone else. We all had to retreat into the formless lifestyle of the solitary.

The group-think of the new way of life was a relief. Selfishly, like a vindicated child watching a repeated mistake by another who didn't heed their warning, I watched and listened as those not directly impacted by the pandemic, like myself, descended into the groaning, bored, monotonous routine of the chronically ill. Most had never dealt with an interminable day, fearing an evening whose darkening had no end, only to be faced with another endless day, another endless night, and the grey fog over the future that never cleared. Uncertainty, panic, paranoia, and grief were suddenly the language of newspapers and politicians, not just my own in a teenage journal, of which the following could well be an extract, filled with similes and clichés as it is.

For years, grief had made my tongue weighty as an anchor, and my mouth moved as a caught fish does on the boards of a boat, with violence, but silent. The water beneath the planks mocks the fish, who is alone but so close to home, and others' gilded talking mocked my words that grumbled like rocks on a cliff face, descending to the sea. My mouth had remained closed for over ten years, like eyes against the sun, wary of opening only to be punished.

Now, I found myself in trepidation as the lockdowns lifted. Not for fear of illness, or fear for others' safety (I am selfish, as I've said), but because I realised I had been exposed. The first exposure was that the lockdowns had little bearing on my life.

My life before lockdown was as frozen as it was during. The second exposure was that I was noticeably unable, or unwilling, to plough through the icy freeze to the joy and freedom now closer on the horizon. I did the mature thing when I realised this, and, on the anniversary of my mother's death, as a grown woman, I ran away.

Abandoning my friends and a birthday weekend of which I was a hosting member, I fled London two days ago with a semi packed bag of too many socks and no pyjamas. I'd awoken in the early afternoon with a head heavy from last night and a heart heavy with last decade's grief. It is better to be lonely alone than lonely in company, so I booked into a hotel on the coast more suited to a crime drama than a self-indulgent escape. A huge, bulking, dirty white monstrosity staring into the sea, with scaffolding on the walls where ivy should have been. I felt caught between compressing walls of humour at my own dramatics and laughter, or perhaps they were wails, travelled through my mouth; the mind is not confined by the realities of physics, but can travel through time and emotion in a matter of skipped heartbeats.

I ate alone in my room and decided that before succumbing to sleep, I would wander into the evening sun for a glass of wine. I found a white lighthouse bar with empty bottles of champagne for vases on each table holding a fresh white rose. A group behind me loudly celebrated an engagement, and I opened the only book I had brought, not currently being enthralled in a fiction: *Hymns, Poems and Prose for Every Occasion*. If these words, which greater eyes than mine had seen and wiser mouths than mine had spoken, had been worth reprinting thousands of times, there must be something in them that could release the rocks that rattled around in my mouth like loose teeth in a dream.

As it was, Shakespeare, Tennyson, Rosetti and St Paul didn't help me. Instead, it was strangers on the table behind me named Clara, Lance, Emily and Chris who did, young and beautiful, all four recently engaged, all four vaccinated, all four celebrating life. Slurring their words and almost falling into the harbour, they became unlikely players in my drama, adding comedy to what I had been thinking of, with on-brand melodrama, as a tragedy.

Emily and Clara came over first. They sat and asked why I was alone. Before the rocks in my mouth had the chance to stick in my throat, I explained that I was grieving my mother and trying to come to terms with how the following day would be the first in which I'd had no mother longer than I'd had one. It is true that grief has no time limit, but if it did, I would have wagered it would end when the two halves of the same sand timer met in the middle, one to continue falling, the other to stop entirely. I found the words were suddenly not rocks, but petals like those of the white roses in the champagne bottles, and they fell on Clara's eyes, which closed as though pressed downwards. She said her father had passed away last year. Their fiancés pulled over two more chairs and yelled out to the cooling harbour that we all had grief, we all had death on our shoulders. Lance's father had died, Chris's mother too and, I felt that this shared grief lifted my own. We high-fived like school children in the same detention and toasted to mothers; those with them left vowed to hug them whenever the chance arose, except Emily, who sipped her champagne, cocked an eyebrow and muttered that her mother encouraged affection about as much as an angry hornet.

Our shouts and laughter summoned the lighthouse keeper, who pulled up a chair and told us how his son had died abroad last year, and how the grief had taken his hope and purpose. How could he be here, then, running a champagne bar with his thespian charisma in a lighthouse, wearing a straw hat and a tattered waistcoat? He took a deep breath, credited his hope to those left to him, his wife and remaining daughter, and said his purpose now was to stop drinks being served to those who sat about on a Saturday night talking about grief. Lance told him his purpose was pointless, to which the lighthouse keeper agreed. He ordered us another bottle of champagne and climbed the steps to his lookout.

The evening settled into the harbour and we sank a few more bottles before a dancing spirit overtook Emily and Clara. We spoke about their relationships, the budding romances of their early twenties, the proposals that had both taken place earlier that week. They talked about their jobs, and their families, and Chris became philosophical, speaking of boats and planks taken apart and whether the nature of a thing is its form or its essence committed unto it by others. I told him to read *Klara and the Sun by Kashuo Ishiguro* if he wanted an answer, and he tried hard to record the name on his notes app with one eye shut. Incoherence joined us shortly after and they decided the local jazz club could use their talents indefinitely into the morning.

Without me realising it, the rocks of grief that had kept me isolated for over a decade were the same ones these strangers now threw to clear the path for my release. I rarely speak of grief, but now that I have, I know it can only lead to more connection. With over a year of constant death, it is grief that will lead us into the next part of the century, that will be the making of the next generation. After war, after famine, after plague, after all the horrors of living, we will connect over grief as surely and repeatedly as the lighthouse torch flickered round the harbour once I was alone again.

Tuesday 15th June 2021: Jamie Backhouse

Reflections are interesting. Not often do we take the time to sit and think about past ventures or happenings. We are either too busy or don't give our thoughts the time to properly process. Some say 'never look back' but I've found it often helps in moving forward.

This is currently my third year of teaching and to say it has been an experience is an understatement. I often hear 'you're not the newbie anymore' but I really think I am! I have only completed one full year with a class after all. However, in some ways I have probably learnt more in these bizarre times than I would have if things were 'normal'.

Teaching obviously has its wonderful perks and insightful moments but oh man, do I need 29 hours sleep or what! Lockdown has made me see just how lucky I was to be in a profession that didn't stop due to the virus. Teachers were needed in various roles and I am grateful I was able to keep doing what I consider myself to be pretty decent at. Whether it be supervising key worker children, teaching online lessons, reading exciting stories to a camera in a strange wig or taking a register in a room by myself (I promise I'm not crazy), teachers have been able to continue to contribute in some way, shape or form.

On the flip side of handwashing, wiping surfaces 16 times an hour and maintaining human bubbles, I have enjoyed finding new catchphrases in my classroom. A new personal favourite motto is 'hands, feet and breath to ourselves please'. It's also surprising how often you can say "Glen please move your mouth away from Mack's face, he doesn't need your germs all over him," in a single day (names changed for professionalism, obviously). And how could I forget the day little Alice (I have swapped names for members of my family) came up to me on the playground to tell me a joke. "Why did the cow cross the road Mr Backhouse?" Alice asked. "I have no idea, why did the cow cross the road Alice?" I listlessly replied, not expecting much. "Well, the cow didn't cross the road... then he killed himself" and proceeded to walk off chuffed that she had indeed managed to make me laugh, at what was such a left field 'joke'. I am currently observing any further jokes she tries to tell for inappropriate content.

As much as I jest, it has also been incredible to witness the resilience and strength of each and every one of my children this year, regardless of their personal experience of the pandemic. Perhaps it's their age-related naivety, or the fact that they were just focused on when the outdoor play parks would open, but I have a newfound respect for children generally. Obviously, it is early days and we won't know the full effect of recent goings on for some time to come, but on the face of it they have shown themselves to be role models in a time when adults often acted in ill-advised, immature, and darn right unbelievable ways.

I am supposed to be writing reports but this was a welcome stalling of something that will no doubt take me a lot longer on my afternoon. But I could not end this entry without mentioning the dedication and adaptability of other gems in the classroom and that's my teaching assistants and support staff generally across UK schools. They are, without doubt, the most necessary and needed asset within the four walls of my classroom and they are often overlooked when teachers are thanked for what they have done for children throughout any given year. They take on all roles necessary to ensure a smoother way through the day and for that I am eternally grateful because I know how rough my day would be without them right there with me. They make me laugh, smile, relax and above all, bring me a banging cup of coffee just when it's needed. This pandemic would have been a lot more stressful without them, and not just at school. Thanks guys!

If you take nothing else from these thoughts, just know that there are some special little people on their way up that will make sure that we are OK in the end.

Wednesday 16th June: Donna Stokes

When lockdown was announced it was actually a personal relief to me. In the months leading up to the announcement I was dreading social engagements, play dates for my children, the school run and anything that meant I had to be in the public eye.

In October 2019 I had received the unexpected diagnosis of breast cancer. This had been a complete and utter shock and I found that the only way I could cope was to continue life as I knew it whilst battling this nightmare privately.

By March 2020, I had lost all my hair and eyelashes and each chemo treatment made me slightly weaker. Wearing a full wig, woolly hat and full eye make-up whilst exchanging banter on the school run was getting harder and harder. I resented the fact that everyone else was going about life normally whilst I was going through such an inhumane treatment. I really don't think I could have got through this without the tremendous support I received from close friends and family which definitely made my battle easier.

At the start of the pandemic, as my immune system was so low, the fear of Covid was high. After my third chemo, an emergency doctor's appointment was needed at the local surgery. However, because of my condition I had to sit in a separate waiting area to wait to be seen. Following the appointment, the doctor, unsure of how to treat me with the looming Covid restrictions, needed to speak with my oncologist and decided the best thing was for me to leave and return in 15 minutes. With torrential rain outside, I found a quiet coffee shop where I was too wary to drink their coffee so I purchased a can of drink and sat in a deserted corner with it unopened till I had the call from the doctor.

Diagnosed with a potential blood clot I was rushed to the hospital. Childcare issues and the threat of Covid meant a frantic text to an old friend to say I was on my way to hospital and asking if she could pick me up as I was too scared to get a taxi. She was totally unaware of the condition but arrived at the hospital immediately. This was an emotional moment I will not forget especially when she saw me without the wig and I received a telling off for not letting her know sooner!

Lockdown did mean I could finally go through this battle privately. Though there was the added fear that the rest of my treatment may be cancelled. Covid meant attending the final two chemo treatments and 10 radiation treatments on my own. It was such an event to get out of the house and see people I took to dressing up in nice clothes for these sessions. When I rang the bell to signify the end of treatment there was no one there to rejoice in that moment with me and I actually had to ask the security guard to take my photo. Celebrations at home meant it could only be with my immediate family and an Indian takeaway!

Our private bubble and lockdown gave me the luxury of recovering from the treatment, there were no deadlines to meet, no school runs to complete, and our garden became an extension of our lounge and hours were spent watching snails, painting walls and general fun times, precious time I will never forget as we became separate from the outside world and counted down the days to the end of treatment.

Being classed as a vulnerable patient, I was unable to go for walks, so I resumed my yoga with a passion and Tabata sessions became a firm favourite.

Online support during this period was invaluable. I joined two Facebook groups for women dedicated to my type of cancer, a support network with a group of local ladies called 'Strong Women' and I formed close attachments with two ladies I met at the hospital and another lady from Kent who was diagnosed the same time as me, in which we shared our journey together.

I definitely feel Covid made our online interaction stronger as we were able to share our experiences together.

Covid only became real to me when I turned on the news at night, the rising figures was terrifying.

As I was unable to go to the shops or outside, internet shopping became a godsend. When I found out I could have my own supermarket delivery slot I was over the moon. I was even eligible for the weekly food hamper too. My partner had to open all my post and a close friend was on call to do all my personal shopping.

As we came out of the lockdown for the first time, I was finally able to celebrate and meet with family. I even went wild swimming twice, which was something I always wanted to do. Swimming in the cold water without my wig was the most invigorating experience. Shortly after I decided to pack the wig away and received many comments regarding my 'drastic haircut' and with Covid I found I did not need to explain.

When the lockdown was announced again at Christmas we were absolutely devastated after what had been such a hard year we had been so looking forward to spending valuable time with our families. Instead, my partner cooked his first Christmas roast and we had a nice walk along the seafront. Face time calls became so precious to us in keeping up to date with family members.

In April 2021 I received the 'all clear' and just two weeks ago I was able to celebrate with friends and family (separate occasions!) properly.

It's now a year since treatment ended and the world became 'quiet'. In a way Covid to me was surreal. Time spent away from family has made me realise how special each day spent together is.

Looking back on the last 12 months I can see now see how fortunate I was. My cancer was diagnosed before the lockdown and my treatment continued throughout. The NHS were fantastic and despite reports of cancer patients lacking support, my treatment was first class and I had the privilege of recovering in my own time with no interruptions from the outside world. I made new friends online and I was even promoted at work to a brand-new role.

It has been a significant part of my life in which I learned valuable life lessons; I will never again take my health for granted. I am eternally grateful for the exceptional kindness I received from both family and friends, especially as I can see now they were all facing their own Covid challenges.

I have learnt to find enjoyment in each new day, if anything this last year has shown us all in some way that none of us really know what the future will bring.

Thursday 17th June 2021: Prabir Mitra

This morning is cloudy; the train compartment I am travelling in is sparsely populated but it is certainly more than I thought it would be. I am travelling to Cambridge, and I am feeling a certain degree of excitement as I have not left my town in over a year, I mean since the beginning of the pandemic. I am feeling good due to regaining 'some degree of normalcy' and also, I am looking forward to examining the final year medical students at the Cambridge Medical School today, face to face, as opposed to last year's online examination. It always gives me positive vibes to see the enthusiasm and determination in the faces of the medical students. It reminds me of my younger days…

As the train left Kings Lynn, I dived into my world of thoughts. I could not help thinking what I did exactly one year back… it was so different, and so distant, that it certainly felt like more than one year, it felt like eternity….

17th June 2020

"How are you doc? Today is the first time that I left my flat in three months" … It was a known voice. I looked closely – the foggy glasses and the mask made it difficult, but I could recognise his face. He was a patient I have known for years. Not many times we, as doctors, receive a greeting asking how 'we' were, but he was different. I smiled and greeted him as I started to examine him in the 'Red Zone' as he had presented with suspected Covid symptoms. I was surprised that he could even recognise me behind my PPE.

The practice regulations were such that any patients who presented with fever or any respiratory symptoms and who needed to be seen by a GP were asked to come to the 'Red Zone' – and in our practice it was a portacabin in the corner of the staff car park that had been turned into a consulting room.

Exactly seventy-seven days previous to this the prime minister had announced something strange called 'lockdown'. It was a new term. As the whole world was fighting this invisible enemy, within a matter of days everyone's priorities had changed, and we were getting used to the new normal. New vocabulary, new dress codes, new ways of working, new ways of greeting – the changes were innumerable.

For us as doctors, we had to adapt to a completely different way of consultation. The 'human-touch' seemed to be a distant dream. Patients also feared to come out their houses and the doctor-patient relationship suddenly faced barriers that included social as well as physical distance. The effects of Covid were so varied and generally so severe that we had found ourselves out of our depths. National and international guidelines were changing rapidly, and it was almost impossible to keep on top of it.

The consultation skills that I had been teaching my GP trainees for years had become so outdated so quickly. With my examiner's hat on, I even signed up with the Cambridge Medical School's initiative to conduct examination of the final year medical students using a remote online platform – assessing and marking students on their skills from my own study - just unbelievable…. SO different but life had to go on…..

17th June 2021
Today, exactly one year later, as I am sitting on the train to Cambridge, I could not stop thinking of what we were going through a year back. The world has changed so much in this last year.

I took a deep breath as the train approached Cambridge station. I was looking forward towards an exciting day ahead.

Friday 18th June 2021: Isabel Varey
Memory and identity

For me, the first lockdown triggered vivid memories of other moments that have marked change in my life – school transitions, changes in friendship groups, definitive times at work. Other moments when routine and expectation have been disrupted.

Standout memories capture overwhelming frustration, others overwhelming gratitude.

However, while some change has been a rollercoaster, some has been marked by its low-key presence and constancy. The low-level anxiety that everything isn't quite 'right', heightened wonder in the natural world, pangs of loss, and new local and virtual connections. Many memories are testament to daily getting-out-of-bed and making sense of the day, or finding calm in the days that did not make much sense at all.

A vivid mix of memories and feelings has given me emotional gauges to the last year, as I realise I have for other stages of my life. These memories and this time are now part of me. As significant as those from teenage years or in my first job – the change triggered by the pandemic has lasted long enough to be a 'stage'.

Real vs virtual

As many others have, I've been going to a virtual office for well over a year. I go through the day's work, decisions, new ideas, breakthroughs, unexpected barriers, and discoveries, in video calls and chats, instant messages, emails, WhatsApp groups, and phone calls.

We have shared worries, optimism, joy and pain over these calls and messages. The people I have worked with virtually during the pandemic know the real me – they have seen a real spectrum of my behaviours and emotional responses, and they have contributed to me developing as a person.

The real vs virtual distinction isn't helpful if the implication is that interactions and connection that happen 'in real life' are intrinsically of more value. I know that the 'virtual' interactions I have had with people during the pandemic have been some of the most real and important I have ever had.

Great work can happen virtually and the professional relationships that develop are genuine and meaningful – individuals and organisations are showing that.

Also, I suspect offices were not always the idea-generating-havens we can be susceptible to conjuring images of them as.

And the office is not our only or best hope of spontaneous interactions …

Being my whole self at home
As I look ahead, I sense that the greatest lasting transition will be that my work 'base' is at home.

That hasn't meant that work now over-reaches and I never shut off from it – in fact, I am even more consciously giving it boundaries.

However, family and friends going through my workday with me has meant that they can be more connected to that side of me, which has felt very positive.

We love to say: 'bring your whole self to work', however in the other direction we only think of work as impinging on the people we want to be at home, distracting us from our families and what 'matters'.

My work self is important to me and I like that I can increasingly 'be my whole self at home'.

My old commute-and-office hours now encompass other activities, such as regularly walking or running with friends and meeting for meals when restrictions have allowed. Plus lunchtimes with my husband, giving us time to talk each day and find links between our work.

More external input into my work-based thoughts has added significantly to my development of new ideas. Will a similar external injection have been critical for other people and organisations responding to the pandemic?

Are workplaces benefiting from a much wider range of external consultants in the form of friends and family now closer to the daily ins-and-outs of each other's work lives? There's a new office kettle, lunchtime chat, corridor walk – in people's homes, local streets, and parks.

And now, as lockdown lifts, this phenomenon may become more visible as it gets easier to meet and interact.

Potential
With all change comes potential – and the pandemic has triggered a huge change. The personal loss and illness has been devastating, now we need to make sure we make the most of the opportunities that have arisen to think differently about how we interact with our world.

Saturday 19th June 2021: Chloe Connor aged 11
Hi, I'm Chloe, I'm 11 years old and I live with my mum, dad, and younger brother Lucas.

Since Covid came life has been unusual.

When we went into lockdown I was a bit unsure what it was going to be like. It all seems a bit of a blur to me now though. The days felt longer because we didn't have as much to do as usual. I had to do my schoolwork at home and I spent the rest of my time either video calling friends and family, going for bike rides and walks in our local neighbourhood (our daily exercise), playing games like Uno, Monopoly and Cluedo. Mum and I discovered TikTok and I played a lot of Xbox with Lucas. Mum and Dad bought a pool for the garden (like so many families in England did last summer) and we had loads of fun playing in that.

Remote learning was definitely the hardest part of lockdown because it was difficult to do my work at home. It was hard to concentrate and Mum and Dad are certainly not teachers, that is for sure! They did reward us with time on the Xbox for hard work though, so we got to have fun when all the learning was done. Sometimes we did things like or baking or art instead of our schoolwork.

The best parts of lockdown were the times when restrictions eased, and we were allowed to meet up with people outside and go to places we hadn't been able to go. We went to the beach a few times and it was a bit strange being around the general public again. Instead of trick or treating we went to a Halloween show in a circus tent, it was fun dressing up and I enjoyed the show too. It was nice to be able meet my friends at the park even if we were only allowed two households to be together. One of my friends came round to our house and we played in the pool. It felt like I hadn't seen her in decades. It was lovely. I'm really grateful to have had the internet and video calling to stay in touch with everyone, even though my grandparents didn't always find it easy to use but that was quite funny.

I was happy when we allowed to go back to school in September 2020. I was looking forward to seeing my friends and doing normal stuff again. Things did change at school like the teachers wearing masks and standing at the front of the classroom, staying in our bubbles, and not mixing with the other kids, windows being open all the time, sanitising hands, no whole-school events, and virtual assemblies but I got used to it after a while. I think that some of the children in my class have forgotten how to behave well because they spent so much time at home.

When I was younger, I always looked forward to being in year six because we would be the oldest in the school and have more responsibilities like being house captains and being role models for the others. The year sixes usually get to go on a residential trip. Unfortunately, Covid and social distancing meant that those things did not happen and that has been disappointing. The teachers have told us that because we've missed our residential, they have a surprise planned for us which is quite exciting! I've got a feeling that it's a party!

So recently I started to feel like things were getting back to normal and then the boy I sit next to in class was sent home, the teachers told us that his parent had Covid. Later that week they heard that the boy had symptoms and that our whole class would need to stay at home the following day. I was sitting in suspense waiting for news and unfortunately, he tested positive. The whole class would now be isolating for 10 days. I felt the most at risk because I sit next to him, but luckily for me I haven't had any symptoms and all my lateral flow tests have been negative. So it has been back to remote learning for me and being stuck at home. Today is my first day out of isolation and it feels great! Even though I haven't really been anywhere today it's just so nice to know that I could go out if I wanted to.

I've been quite lucky because not many of my family members have caught the virus and I know that lots of people have not been so lucky as me.

I am very much looking forward to a day when I can go out with my friends and family without wearing masks or worrying about social distancing. Although I think that hand sanitisers in public places should stay to keep all the germs away all the time.

From this whole experience I feel that we have all realised how important our friends and family are and how to love the little things in life a little more.

Sunday 20th June 2021: Mark Warwick

Like most of us I was kind of gobsmacked and floored when the Covid-19 pandemic first manifested in March 2020, none of us could have expected the aftermath or the huge changes that were to come – 15 months on I am more than happy to document my thoughts for prosperity.

So, March 2020 I was personally in quite a dark place just coming through a 22-year marriage separation, some close non Covid related deaths, financial burdens, changing jobs, adjusting to single life, fighting my own recovery demons, and trying to rebuild relationships with my children who are the world to me. At the time Covid-19 was really the last thing I needed….

Two options I guess, give up or crack on – I chose the latter.

To me the most important thing was the health and safety of my children and my own spirit. My working practices changed from lots of on-site work, mainly based around Bristol to working full time alone from home (though with the remote backup from my team and company).

On a work note, this worked well for me as I am geographically based over 200 miles from my location so the first positive for me from the pandemic was the ability to be very close (under a mile) from my children. Their mother was keen for me to help and have them as much as possible and that was the start of something beautiful and now, 15 months on, I have such a strong relationship with them that is truly a blessing, whereas before I was often a long way away for periods of time for work.

Like any separated father, my children do not live with me so my next plan of action was to ensure I could fill my spare time alone with things to do.

I forgot things like how much I enjoyed drawing after the confidence I'd had as a teen had taken a 30-year hiatus. I'm not great but in the early days I did many lead drawings of buildings and landscapes but only for friends that the pictures had meaning for so that was a double win for me, keeping occupied and also giving a little smile to some people that were also worried to death about what was going on.

I picked up my guitar for the first time in years and although not great, got many hours of enjoyment out of that too.

I am a keen motorcyclist so spend many evenings on my own riding out to secluded coves to help with my spiritual recovery from my past and to help me try and understand what was going on. Lamorna cove is southwest Cornwall and to this day still remains 'my place' where I go to ponder the answers of life. I remember in around May 2020 (my birthday alone) sitting there one evening, there was not a soul about, the sea was glass flat and the sky unbroken blue, a couple of seals and a dolphin were playing in the water and I could not help but think this was Mother Nature's way of healing herself after years of abuse.

I so totally understand that so many people have lost so much through this awful pandemic but I also believe that if you look hard enough there is good under every stone and for me that good has been the ability to be closer to my children, my understanding of myself better as a person, and my gratitude for being alive and being able to reach out to people and help.

I am the kind of person that has no room in my life any more for negativity or nasty people and the lovely things this heightened in me was the ability to accept life on life's terms. The humility and gratitude that although I - like many others - have been through hard times, there is always someone worse off than yourself. And I guess, most importantly, the genuine passion to be kind, helpful, and considerate of others. I was never a horrible person but now I feel I am a spiritually 'better' person than I was before the pandemic began.

We are still in the throes of the situation so who knows how and when this ends but the life lessons I have learnt of tolerance, gratitude, humility, respect, and mindfulness will remain with me for the rest of my life and I will in a strange way (with reflection) be grateful I lived through the pandemic and what it taught me. You cannot buy understanding or gratitude so I will remain ever thankful and I am most grateful to Michelle for giving me the opportunity to document my thoughts.

Though not religious in the traditional way, I pray every morning and night now for my children, those that I love, those that continue to suffer and for the heath and sanity of people that are close to me and every 24 hours just try to be the best person I can. *'God grant me the serenity to accept the things I cannot change, the courage to change the things that I can and the wisdom to know the difference'.*

Take care all and thanks for reading.

Monday 21st June 2021: Michelle Gant

21st June 2021. Summer solstice. The longest day. And of course, what had once been badged as 'Freedom Day'.

Freedom Day was going to be the day when all the restrictions that have loosened and tightened over the last year were removed. When we could hug with abandon, when we could stop keeping our distance, when we could gather together more easily once more. Of course, a new variant and rising cases has put paid to that happening for the time being. Now, we're keeping one eye over the horizon to 19th July and another eye fixed on those rising cases.

I cringe every time I hear the phrase Freedom Day (ditto: the 'new normal', another term thrown up in this Coronavirus era). Because whilst I know that the continued restrictions will no doubt be having an impact on so many – and my heart goes out to those businesses and people affected – in some ways, the lessons we've learnt over the last year can be liberating.

As the saying goes 'necessity is the mother of invention' and wow, hasn't that been the case since 2020. I sit here today fully vaccinated: just 24 hours ago, I had my second jab, delivered thanks to our amazing NHS staff and volunteers. This is a vaccine that didn't exist 18 months ago, that has only been rolled out over the last six months or so, to tackle a disease that none of us knew about before we started reading and hearing about in early 2020. *Covid what?* I am in grateful awe of the scientists, the medical staff, and everyone else who made this happen.

But not just the vaccine, as incredible a feat that is. Across the world, we have adapted en masse in response to the virus. There are so many things that we thought couldn't be done pre-Covid that we've shown actually, they can be. Not least in the world of work. Because of the circumstances that we've found ourselves in, we've liberated our thinking and that freedom has led to some of the most brilliant creativity and innovation that has helped us to live and work and carry on. I hope we retain that innovative adaptability and know without a doubt that we can do anything. Just look at us, just look at everything we've done! We're amazing – and capable of anything.

In many ways, we've also been freed to be ourselves. We've seen into each other's worlds – not least when a family member wanders into shot on screen! And we've talked to each other with perhaps more depth than we might once have done – really talked about how we're feeling. When we're struggling, when we're having a bad day. We've dared to share of ourselves, because of this thing we're all living through. How freeing it has been to just be us: low points, bad days, and all. I hope we retain that too. I hope that we can come out of this and just be ourselves, our whole, authentic selves. And know that we are fantastically perfect, utterly wonderful just as we are.

I hope too that the last year has liberated us to not to be afraid to follow our dreams – big or small – and live the lives that we want. There has been so much tragedy, pain, anguish, and despair and as so many of the amazing contributors When The World Paused have commented, it's brought the realisation that life is utterly precious. So why spend it doing what we think we 'should' do or what everyone else is doing: there's a great saying I heard recently: 'don't measure your progress using someone else's ruler'. Do what makes you happy: you deserve it.

The other thing that has happened in the last year is we've found gratitude for the small stuff. Like the mist clearing on a foggy day, the things that we took for granted suddenly became that which our hearts most desired. They had always been there, we just hadn't valued them as much as the big shiny things. But now, lockdown and Covid have suddenly brought all those things into sharp focus. I cannot tell you how amazing it was to hug my mum and dad after a whole year – but I suspect most of you know that feeling. We've been set free: we now know that there's magic in the everyday. How lucky are we?

Perhaps too we've found it easier to show love and kindness. Maybe saying 'I love you' more often. Maybe lending a hand. Maybe offering a gentle word of encouragement when once we'd have looked the other way in shyness. If the pandemic has freed us up to love more and say aloud those feelings once only expressed in our heads, then more power to us. The world needs more of that, always.

Thank you
Covid isn't over. And it won't be over until it's over for everyone: globally, the war has not been won, far from it. And for many, many millions of people, the pain will go on: the numbers of people lost are mind boggling and utterly heartbreaking, especially when you know that every single person is someone who was loved. My thoughts are with all those who were lost and all those who have been left behind: may you find comfort.

As I think back over the last year, I – like so many others have said so beautifully through this journal – feel utterly grateful. That my family for the most part have remained well, to have my own health, and to have not experienced some of the horrors that I have read about.

Thank you. For my family, for my friends, for people who I have connected with in a multitude of ways, for strangers who have shown me kindness, for those who have taken care of us all – from the NHS heroes to key workers everywhere. Thank you.

In my own world, I've been utterly inspired by my darling daughter Thea. Her resilience, her positivity, her gentle good humour is incredible. Our amazing bond has only been strengthened by the many days we've spent together over the last year, making up games that have led to family 'in-jokes' which will sustain us for years to come. Thank you sweetheart for always making the days brighter in the darkest of times.

And my husband, Bobby, who decided in the middle of the pandemic to start training and learning new skills whilst also home-schooling our daughter full-time – you have never been afraid of following the path less travelled. More than that though, his innate goodness, his kindness, his ability to see the best in everything and everyone; thank you for being one of life's good guys.

My wonderful family and beautiful friends who have always been there virtually when I need them. Thank you. I must give a special shout out to my mum who has been shielding for the longest time and who has never once been anything but positive and accepting. She has not complained once. Not once. I wish I could be more like her.

Thank you, thank you, thank you to all the amazing people who have shared their reflections on When The World Paused. Thank you for your candour. Your words have moved me, made me laugh, made me cry, and made me think. And made me feel less alone. I am forever grateful that you shared of yourselves in words. If you have found writing has given you succour, I hope you find it again when you need it.

And thank you too for reading.

What a pandemic taught me about living
The pandemic has taught me that life can change in a heartbeat so just go with it and let it be whatever it's going to be. I have spent a lot of time trying to mould and shape things the way I want them to be rather than just accepting life, warts, and all. I've kidded myself for years that I'm in control – not a bit of it.

I'm just going to deal with whatever gets chucked at me. Because I'm ready for anything.

As we all are.

And I know without a shadow of a doubt that life right here, right now is beautiful. It's amazing. And yet, so often I've thought about what's coming next rather than just enjoying this moment. No more. Every bit of it, I'm just going to love it and make the most of it.

Carpe diem.

Wherever you are, whenever it is that you're reading this, may you be happy and may you be healthy. Because as the last year has taught us, that's absolutely everything. It really is.

Index of contributors:
Allen, Steph: 129 - 131
Backhouse, Jamie: 238 - 240
Bartlett, Clive: 141 - 143
Bishop, Donna-Louise: 66 - 69
Brighton, Stephanie: 73 - 76
Brown, Gemma: 210 - 211
Buchan, Fiona: 174 - 176
Burrows, Kate: 198 - 199
Carver, Haze: 206 - 209
Clarke, Robert: 33 - 34
Clifton, Sharon: 87 - 90
Cluett, Emma: 105 - 107
Coathup, Jodi: 161 - 162
Connor, Chloe: 250 - 252
Davis, Stephani: 180 - 182
Dennis, Sarah: 93 - 95
DW: 44 - 45
Etheridge, Vicky: 41 - 43
Fawcett, Caroline: 146 - 148
Findlay, Claire: 17 - 24
Fox, Ange: 96 - 98
Francis, Anne: 15 - 16
Franklin, Anna: 120 - 122
Freeman, Hannah: 108 - 112
Fry, Jacqueline: 132 - 133
Gant, Michelle: 7; 8 - 12; 256 - 260
Gant, Robert: 203 - 205
Gant, Thea: 134 - 135
Gant, Wendy: 183 - 184
Grant, Serena: 99 - 101
Hales, Martin: 80 - 83
Hall, Tony: 91 - 92
Hamer, Anita: 189 - 190
Haverson, Vicki: 222 - 224
Haysman, Stu: 35 - 37
Holmes, Georgie: 196 - 197

Holt, Peter: 25 - 27
Holt, Tom: 231 - 233
Hooper, Helen: 53 - 55
Jackson, Ronda: 70 - 72
Jonas, Kirsty: 115 - 117
Jones, Sarah: 149 - 151
Laing, Lara: 113 - 114
Lawson, Gill: 118 - 119
Lawson, Lucy: 187 - 188
Lake, Jo: 177 - 179
Li, Sauy: 38 - 40
Liverpool, Candice: 200 - 202
McGurk, Jayne: 168 - 170
Mitra, Prabir: 245 - 246
Murray, Edward: 220 - 221
Murray, Thomas: 139 - 140
O'Shaughnessy, Emma: 61 - 62
Outten, Emma: 228 - 230
Page, Tom: 56 - 57
Panks, Abbie: 51 - 52
Playford, Chris: 58 - 60
Playford, Jo: 13 - 14
Pritchard, Nicola: 28 - 29
Purves, Charley: 30 - 32
Robinson, Janka: 144 - 145
Rouse, Georgina: 77 - 79
Sexton, Charlotte: 159 - 160
Sheren, Alma: 126 - 128
Shield, Julie: 171 - 173
Siewniak, Michal: 46 - 50
Slusar, Samantha: 152 - 153
Smith, Claire: 166 - 167
Staveley, Neil: 84 - 86
Stokes, Donna: 241 - 244
Terry, Helen: 63 - 65
Traynor, Janet: 225 - 227
Tydeman, Anna: 154 - 158

Varey, Isabel: 247 - 249
Walden, Rosie: 136 - 138
Warden, Eliza: 234 - 237
Warman, Danielle: 185 - 186
Warwick, Mark: 253 - 255
Weeks, Liam: 191 - 195
West-Burnham, Eddie: 212 - 215
Wigley, Lucy: 102 - 104
Wharton, Johnny: 163 - 165
Wood, Suzanna: 216 - 219
Young, Alix: 123 - 125

References:
44: von Franz, Marie-Louise: 'The Problem of The Puer Aeternus' – first published 1970
45: Wyndham, John: 'The Day of The Triffids' – first published 1951
91: 'Dark Waters' released 2019 directed by Todd Haynes
131: Mackesy, Charlie: 'The Boy, The Mole, The Fox, and The Horse' – first published 2019
143: 'Perfect Circle' performed by Mega City Four. Composed by Wiz, label Big Life. Released 1994.
150: Hollins, Peter: 'The Science of Self-Discipline' – first published 2017
224: Hone, Lucy: 'The Three Secrets of Resilient People' – TedX Christchurch, August 2019
225: 'Listen to the Music' performed by the Doobie Brothers. Songwriter Tom Johnston, label Warner Bros. Released 1972.
225: Scientific Reports 18/02/21 via The Telegraph
225: 'Sunshine' performed by Gabrielle. Songwriters Gabrielle and Jonathan Shorten, label Go1 Beat. Released 1999.
225: 'Miss You' performed by the Rolling Stones. Songwriters Jagger-Richards, label Rolling Stones. Released 1978.
225: 'Waiting on a War' performed by The Foo Fighters. Songwriters Dave Grohl, Taylor Hawkins, Rami Jaffee, Nate Mendel, Chris Shiflett, Pat Smear, label RCA, released 2021.
225: 'American Patrol' performed by Glen Miller Orchestra. Arranged by Jerry Gray, Victor Records, released 1942.
225: 'Boogie Woogie Bugle Boy' performed by The Andrews Sisters. Songwriters Don Raye and Hughie Prince, Studio Decca, Hollywood, California, recorded 1941.
225: 'Good Times' performed by Chic. Songwriters Bernard Edwards and Nile Rodgers, label Atlantic. Released 1979.
225: 'Summer Nights' performed by John Travolta & Olivia Newton-John. Songwriters Jim Jacobs and Warren Casey, label RSO. Released 1978.
225: 'Perfect Day' performed by Lou Reed. Songwriter Lou Reed, label RCA. Released 1972.

226: 'Lovely Day' performed by Bill Withers. Songwriters Bill Withers and Skip Scarborough, label Columbia. Released 1977.
226: 'Sunny Afternoon' performed by The Kinks. Songwriter Ray Davies, labels Pye (UK) and Reprise (US). Released 1966.
226: 'It's Raining Men' performed by The Weather Girls. Songwriters Paul Jabara and Paul Shaffer, labels CBS, Columbia. Released 1982.
226: 'Make Me Smile (Come Up and See Me)' performed by Steve Harley. Songwriter Steve Harley, label EMI. Released 1975.
226: 'Rock the Boat (The Hues Corporation Song)' performed by Hues Corporation. Songwriter Wally Holmes, label RCA Records. Released 1974.
226: 'Glorious' performed by Andreas Johnson. Songwriter Andreas Johnson, label WEA. Released 1999.
226: 'Sir Duke' performed by Stevie Wonder. Songwriter Stevie Wonder, label Tamla. Released 1977.
226: 'Rockin' in the Free World' performed by Neil Young. Songwriter Neil Young, label Reprise. Released 1989.
226: 'We Have All the Time in the World' performed by Louis Armstrong. Songwriters Hal David and John Barry, label Warner Bros. Released 1969.
235: Brandreth, Giles: 'Hymns, Poems, and Prose for all Occasions' – first published 2011.
237: Ishiguro, Kazuo: 'Klara and the Sun' – first published 2021.

Your reflections:

Please use this space to capture your own reflections on what happened for you When The World Paused – and what a pandemic taught you about living.

Printed in Great Britain
by Amazon